VISIONS OF ANCIENT LEICESTER

Reconstructing life in the Roman and medieval town from the archaeology of the Highcross Leicester excavations

Mathew Morris, Richard Buckley and Mike Codd

University of Leicester Archaeological Services (ULAS) is a unit of professional archaeologists based within the School of Archaeology and Ancient History at the University of Leicester. ULAS undertakes archaeological projects all over the UK, mostly connected with planning applications for new developments, road schemes and quarries. The unit has particular expertise in urban archaeology, and staff have been involved in almost all of the major excavations that have taken place in Leicester over the past 35 years.

ULAS, School of Archaeology and Ancient History, University Road, Leicester LE1 7RH

Web: www.le.ac.uk/ulas Email: ulas@le.ac.uk

The **School of Archaeology and Ancient History** is one of the top departments in the UK in terms of teaching, research and student satisfaction. Undergraduate and post-graduate programmes are offered and the school also has a large and thriving Distance Learning community who study at Certificate, undergraduate, Masters and PhD level. Staff have field projects all over the world exploring the archaeologies of past societies from prehistoric through to early modern times. ULAS and the School together run an annual training excavation for students, for many years at Abbey Park in Leicester, but since 2010, at the Iron Age hillfort of Burrough Hill in Leicestershire.

School of Archaeology and Ancient History, University Road, Leicester LE1 7RH

Web: www.le.ac.uk/departments/archaeology Email: arch-anchist@le.ac.uk

Contents

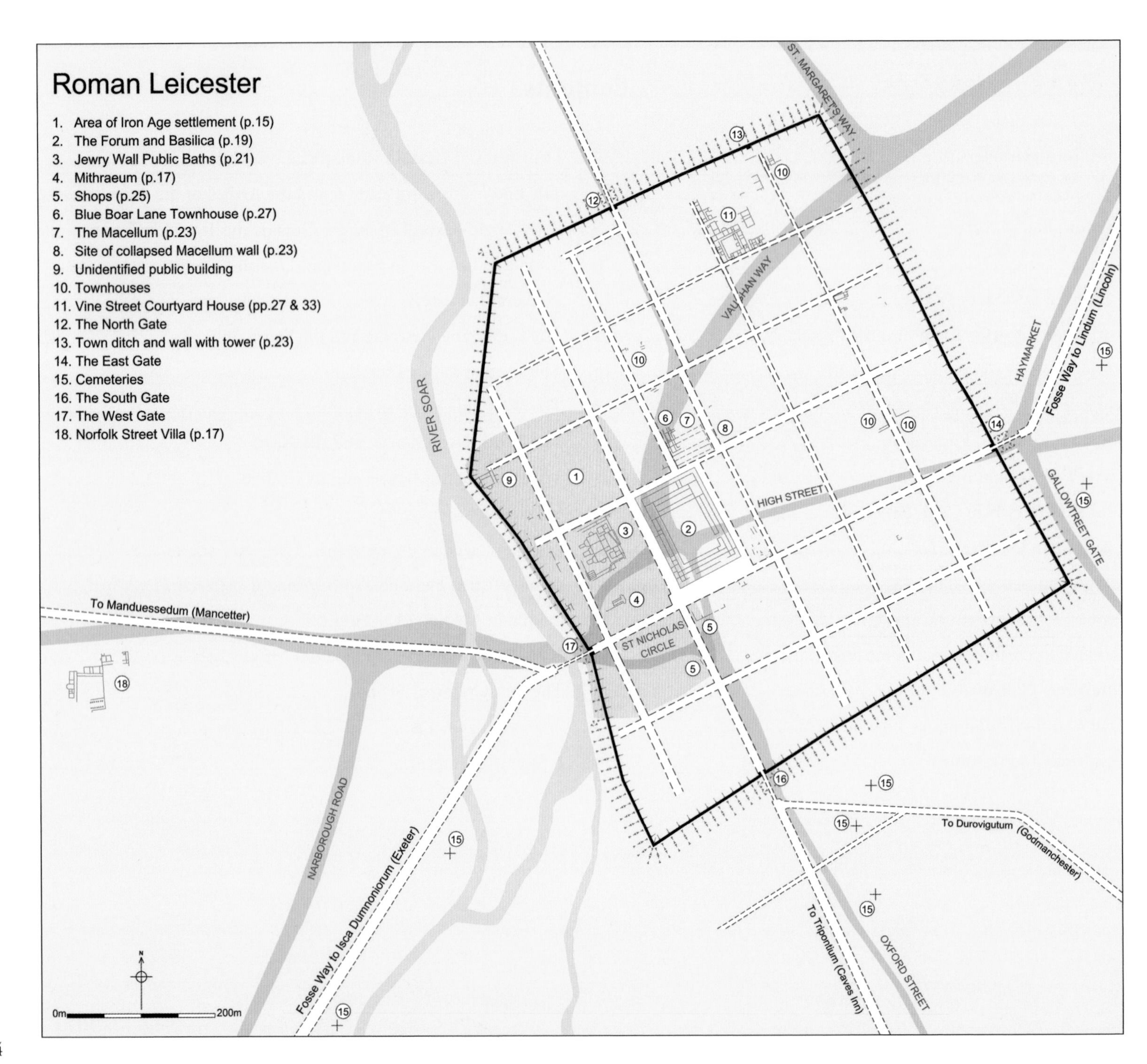

Roman Leicester
1. Area of Iron Age settlement (p.15)
2. The Forum and Basilica (p.19)
3. Jewry Wall Public Baths (p.21)
4. Mithraeum (p.17)
5. Shops (p.25)
6. Blue Boar Lane Townhouse (p.27)
7. The Macellum (p.23)
8. Site of collapsed Macellum wall (p.23)
9. Unidentified public building
10. Townhouses
11. Vine Street Courtyard House (pp.27 & 33)
12. The North Gate
13. Town ditch and wall with tower (p.23)
14. The East Gate
15. Cemeteries
16. The South Gate
17. The West Gate
18. Norfolk Street Villa (p.17)
ST. MARGARET'S WAY
VAUGHAN WAY
RIVER SOAR
HAYMARKET
Fosse Way to Lindum (Lincoln)
HIGH STREET
GALLOWTREE GATE
To Manduessedum (Mancetter)
ST NICHOLAS CIRCLE
NARBOROUGH ROAD
Fosse Way to Isca Dumnoniorum (Exeter)
To Durovigutum (Godmanchester)
To Tripontium (Caves Inn)
OXFORD STREET
N
0m
200m

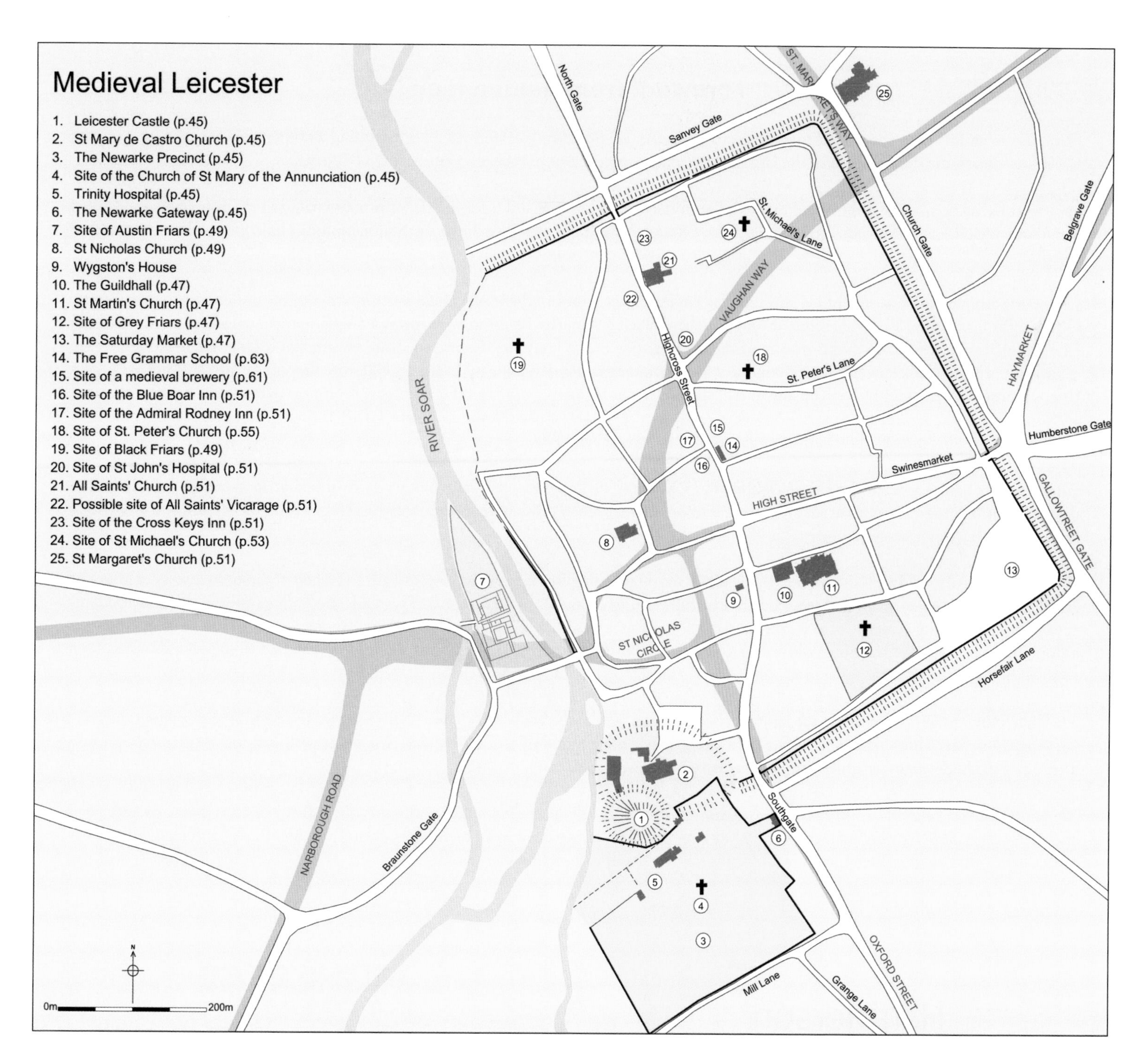

Medieval Leicester
1. Leicester Castle (p.45)
2. St Mary de Castro Church (p.45)
3. The Newarke Precinct (p.45)
4. Site of the Church of St Mary of the Annunciation (p.45)
5. Trinity Hospital (p.45)
6. The Newarke Gateway (p.45)
7. Site of Austin Friars (p.49)
8. St Nicholas Church (p.49)
9. Wygston's House
10. The Guildhall (p.47)
11. St Martin's Church (p.47)
12. Site of Grey Friars (p.47)
13. The Saturday Market (p.47)
14. The Free Grammar School (p.63)
15. Site of a medieval brewery (p.61)
16. Site of the Blue Boar Inn (p.51)
17. Site of the Admiral Rodney Inn (p.51)
18. Site of St. Peter's Church (p.55)
19. Site of Black Friars (p.49)
20. Site of St John's Hospital (p.51)
21. All Saints' Church (p.51)
22. Possible site of All Saints' Vicarage (p.51)
23. Site of the Cross Keys Inn (p.51)
24. Site of St Michael's Church (p.53)
25. St Margaret's Church (p.51)
North Gate
Sanvey Gate
Church Gate
Belgrave Gate
St. Michael's Lane
VAUGHAN WAY
Highcross Street
St. Peter's Lane
HAYMARKET
Humberstone Gate
Swinesmarket
HIGH STREET
GALLOWTREE GATE
RIVER SOAR
ST NICHOLAS CIRCLE
Horsefair Lane
Southgate
NARBOROUGH ROAD
Braunstone Gate
OXFORD STREET
Mill Lane
Grange Lane
0m
200m
N

Foreword from Hammerson

Hammerson and its joint venture partners at launch, Hermes, are proud to have formed an outstanding working relationship with Leicester University during the development of the largest regeneration project ever to take place in the city of Leicester.

Hammerson has been at the forefront of many of the largest and most successful retail-led city-centre regeneration projects across the United Kingdom, including Bullring in Birmingham, The Oracle in Reading and West Quay in Southampton. Highcross in Leicester was no exception.

Our relationship with University of Leicester Archaeological Services, one of the leading field units in the country and one we were extremely fortunate to have at our disposal, began through Richard Buckley. Shortly afterwards we formed a development agreement with Leicester City Council to develop land in the vicinity of the city's existing Shires Shopping Centre to create the region's leading retail and leisure-led destination, Highcross Leicester. The £350 million, 1 million square foot development created a 120 store shopping centre, anchored by John Lewis, House of Fraser and Debenhams, with the leisure element focused around developing a new exterior public square, St Peter's Square, anchored by Showcase Cinema de Lux, 15 restaurants and cafes, as well as the restoration of the Grade II listed Old Grammar School. Over 2,500 jobs were also created upon launch of the scheme in September 2008.

Following the completion of demolition works, the University of Leicester team had full access to the land in question and through a detailed phasing programme, excavated the site and recorded finds where applicable, before construction work began. At one point, over 100 professional archaeologists were involved in this process.

What this particular study has uncovered, is one of the most rewarding Roman archaeological finds in Leicester's modern history, with many artefacts and building structures discovered that had previously been lost or undetected. The finds are both extraordinary and thought-provoking, uncovering evidence of what the everyday lives of the city's earliest inhabitants involved. Amongst some of the startling finds was a Roman Town House with central courtyard on the John Lewis Car Park site, the first time a complete plan of a Roman building has been revealed in the city.

This incredibly insightful record by the University of Leicester is one we are pleased to be associated with. In addition to providing the city's current population with a retail and leisure destination they can be proud of, the activity has also unearthed some of the country's greatest archaeological finds, many of which might never have been discovered.

We would like to congratulate Richard Buckley and his team for their incredible results and thank them for their hard work, commitment and their insight into creating the best possible working practices during the development period, ensuring the Roman and medieval history of Leicester could be documented and recorded for the city to enjoy for many years to come.

Hammerson on behalf of the Highcross Limited Partnership

Preface

This book brings to life Leicester's vibrant past from the earliest settlement 2000 years ago to the 16th century, interpreting the exciting archaeological discoveries of recent years and the stories they tell through the artwork of Mike Codd. One of the most evocative ways of presenting the past is through vivid reconstructions of places as the people who lived, worked and died there would have experienced them. Working closely with archaeologists and historians, Mike has made the buried remains of the ancient city come to life, opening windows onto landscapes and events concealed by the erosion of time.

The drawings in this book represent the culmination of seven years of archaeological research, starting with the major excavations that took place in the first decade of the new millennium as the modern city centre was redeveloped, followed by months of detailed analysis and interpretation of the evidence at the University of Leicester, and culminating in the presentation and display of the discoveries at museums such as the Jewry Wall Museum. Mike's reconstructions also draw on the pioneering work of archaeologists like Kathleen Kenyon, who excavated the Jewry Wall Roman baths in the 1930s, and Jean Mellor, who recorded many sites in the 1960s and 70s at the heart of Roman and medieval Leicester.

This book also illustrates vividly the way the past plays a part in the present. As our city continues to evolve, successive new developments provide both an opportunity to learn about what life was like in the past – and the challenge and necessity of setting the archaeological discoveries on record for the benefit of future generations before they are destroyed forever. The redevelopment of the Highcross quarter in particular afforded an unprecedented opportunity to investigate a significant area of the historic core of the city, through a model partnership with Hammerson, which enabled the archaeologists to record and so preserve the changing story of the quarter from its earliest times, without hindering the building work. Most of the early excavations, whilst collectively important, were small scale and individually provided frustratingly tantalising glimpses of the past city, often raising as many questions as they answered.

It is clear that Leicester was a significant place from the first permanent settlement at the end of the Iron Age. It was an important regional administrative centre in Roman times and developed into a thriving medieval market town, a tradition which the newly expanded retail quarter continues to this day. Some of the new discoveries – like the collapsed Roman wall described below – have been spectacular, others more mundane – simple vestiges of the inhabitants' everyday lives – but all have required painstaking work to reveal their secrets. It has been a privilege for us at the University of Leicester's Archaeological Services and the School of Archaeology and Ancient History to play our part in this project, and by helping to explore the archaeology of the city and the wider region an opportunity for us to give something back in return to the community that sustains and supports the University.

The new understanding generated by the Highcross Leicester development has dramatically enhanced our knowledge, making possible the new synthesis of Leicester's history that is presented here. We hope that *Visions of Ancient Leicester* will appeal to inhabitants and visitors, students and teachers, children and adults alike, and will encourage people to examine and enjoy Leicester's 2000 year heritage.

Professor Colin Haselgrove FBA
School of Archaeology and Ancient History
University of Leicester

3
6
5
7
8
1
4
2

Introduction

Although there is not much above ground today to remind us, Leicester is an ancient city. It first emerged a little over 2000 years ago as the tribal capital of the people known as the *Corieltavi*. Following the Roman invasion of Britain in AD 43, the place continued to prosper, expanding into an important Roman town, *Ratae Corieltavorum*, which lasted for over 350 years. Rapid decline came after the Roman withdrawal in 410 and most of its buildings fell into ruin, but by 680 Leicester had become a religious centre of the Anglo-Saxon Kingdom of Mercia. It briefly fell under the sway of the Danish Vikings between 877 and 918, becoming one of their Five Boroughs (fortified towns) along with Derby, Lincoln, Nottingham and Stamford. After the Norman Conquest of England in 1066, Leicester established itself as an affluent county town. With the arrival of the canal and railway in the 18th and 19th centuries the town became an important industrial centre, particularly for textiles, and in 1919 it was formally granted city status again.

In recent years, a large part of Leicester's historic core has undergone a renaissance. Many industrial buildings of the 1960s and 1970s have been demolished and the land redeveloped for commercial and residential use, giving archaeologists a rare chance to investigate comparatively large areas of the Roman and medieval town in advance of building work. Excavation on this scale is often impossible in many of Britain's ancient towns and cities – particularly those which never became industrialised and still have the layout of medieval streets and properties preserved. In Leicester, the south-eastern quarter of the walled town is largely inaccessible to archaeologists, as this is where the medieval street pattern and many high-quality buildings of the 18th to 20th centuries survive (**1**).

Between 2003 and 2009, University of Leicester Archaeological Services (ULAS) was able to undertake some of the most significant excavations Leicester has ever seen. These ranged across the city from De Montfort University's campus in the south (**2**) to the Leicester Square development on Sanvey Gate in the north (**3**); on Bath Lane (**4**) to the west, and along important historic streets such as Northgate Street (**5**); but by far the single biggest development has been the extension of the former Shires shopping centre into the Highcross Leicester retail quarter (outlined in orange). This occupies approximately five hectares, nearly 10% of the walled Roman and medieval town.

Left: Leicester in 2005, looking north-east across the historic core of the modern city (outlined in red), showing the area earmarked for the new Highcross Leicester development (in orange).

The archaeological work at Highcross started in 2002 with historical research, followed in 2003-4 by several trial excavations designed to find out where archaeological remains were likely to survive and to assess how they would be affected by the building work. In some areas, the archaeology had either been completely destroyed in the past, or was so deeply buried (up to 4m below present street level in places) that it could be left in place undisturbed. However, on three sites, it was clear that archaeological remains would be damaged by the foundations for the new buildings and would need to be carefully excavated to create a record for the benefit of future generations. These were Vine Street (**6**), now beneath the new multi-storey John Lewis car park; on the site of the former St Margaret's Baths on Vaughan Way (**7**), now beneath the John Lewis store; and land along the Highcross Street frontage adjacent to the former Free Grammar School building (**8**).

Since the excavations finished in 2006, detailed examination of the results has been carried out by various specialists at the University of Leicester. Artefacts have been analysed to explore the lifestyle of the past inhabitants – providing clues as to date, wealth, social status and trade. Study of the environmental material and human remains has provided information on the age, sex, diet and health of the people and the nature of the urban landscape in which they lived. Materials such as brick, tile and slate help us to determine the appearance of buildings in the past and the techniques used in their construction.

These results have now been brought together here to paint a detailed picture of how people have lived in Leicester over the past 2000 years and it is this wealth of new information that has allowed us to reconstruct how Leicester may have once looked, from the town's prehistoric origins to the birth of the modern city.

*Right: The handle of a folding Roman clasp knife in the shape of a dog, found at Vine Street (**5**). Reproduced at actual size.*

Excavating in Leicester

Archaeologists encounter a variety of challenges when excavating in Leicester – from working on busy building sites to discovering human remains – but perhaps one of the greatest practical difficulties is the sheer volume of soil and rubble which has to be shifted to reach the archaeology in the first place. In the past, the area occupied by the Highcross Leicester Shopping Centre was not always as built-up as it is today. For long periods of time between the 15th century and the 19th century, the area was used as fields and orchards and these have left over two metres of garden soil covering the Roman and medieval town. Since the 19th century, new houses, factories and offices have also caused further build-up until today the Roman city lies up to four metres beneath our feet.

Top left: An archaeologist supervises the removal of soil whilst the John Lewis store is built around him.

Bottom left: Two mechanical diggers are used to remove the remains of modern buildings and thick layers of garden soil from Vine Street, the site of the new Highcross car park.

Below: Medieval human remains are encountered whist removing garden soil on Vine Street.

Once the garden soil has been carefully removed by mechanical excavator, the archaeologist's work really begins. Excavating urban sites is one of the most complicated jobs in archaeology. This is because two thousand years of human activity, confined in a limited space, has resulted in the build-up of a complex, overlapping sequence of layers ('stratigraphy'). In order to understand this, archaeologists individually label, plan, photograph and record every feature and deposit before they are excavated to collect finds, environmental samples and any other information which will help to identify their date and function. Once analysis of all the evidence has been completed, archaeologists are able to isolate and examine every minute phase and change of activity and so create a detailed narrative of how a site was used over time. By the end of the excavations beneath Highcross Leicester, over 15,000 features and deposits and 1,500 human burials had been unearthed and over 110,000 individual finds were recovered.

People often ask why the archaeology we uncover cannot be preserved and displayed for everyone to see. This is because the remains we find are usually very fragmentary and it is rare to encounter walls, floors and other structures that are in good-enough condition to conserve. In the past, building materials were constantly recycled and often we can only detect the lines of walls by what are known as 'robber trenches' – foundation trenches from which all stone has been removed for re-use. Buildings made of organic materials, such as timber and thatch, mostly do not survive at all and can only be recognised from post-holes dug to take timber uprights or slots for horizontal beams.

Top right: Excavating the remains of the charnel house of St Peter's Church on Vaughan Way. This was used in the medieval period for the storage of skeletons disturbed by building works. The human bones were stacked up in a building whose walls were completely robbed of their stone in the 16th century, leaving a 'robber trench'.

Bottom right: Roman and medieval features survived on Highcross Street, including a substantial part of a collapsed Roman wall (bottom left of photograph)

*The Vine Street site, showing the excavation (**above**), the outline of a large Roman townhouse (**below**), and its reconstruction based on the final results of the excavation (**right**). Reaching this final stage has taken seven years of intensive study involving the expertise of 123 professional archaeologists, 64 volunteers and 36 specialists.*

Reconstructing Leicester's Past

Archaeological reconstruction is an imperfect science. It is impossible to create an exact representation of what was once there, but we can use all the available evidence to show what was most likely to have been there. This is a painstaking process involving considerable feedback between archaeologist and artist. For example, with a building, the archaeologist first uses the excavation records to work out its plan at a particular time and interpret as far as possible the function of various rooms. Clues in the building's plan show where gable-ends were, which walls were structural, their height, and whether the building was single or multi-storeyed. From this, the artist can then produce an initial drawing showing how the superstructure may have appeared.

Stone, slate, tile and plaster recovered during the excavation can also indicate how the building was constructed and what it would have looked like. Finally, where bits of information are missing, the gaps can be filled in by looking at other similar Roman or medieval buildings, in Leicester and elsewhere in Britain.

Once this framework has been established, finer details can be added. The decoration of individual rooms can be reconstructed from fragments of painted wall plaster and flooring materials. Trees, shrubs and crops can be added to the surrounding landscape based on environmental remains; people, clothes, adornments, objects and furniture can all be depicted based on the finds left behind, as can activities and occupations.

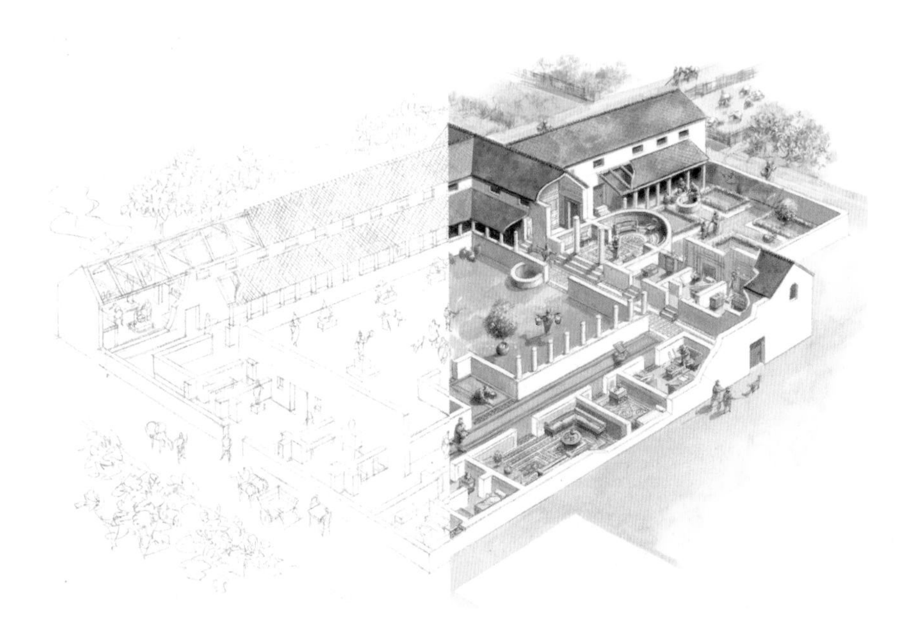

The North-East Quarter Today

Right: The former 16th-century Free Grammar School building is today a restaurant in the Highcross Leicester Shopping Centre. The Highcross Street excavation was carried out around this building.

Bottom left: Looking north across Vaughan Way to the John Lewis multi-storey car park. This was the site of the Vine Street excavation.

Bottom right: Looking west from Causeway Lane to the John Lewis store. This was the site of the Vaughan Way excavation.

Above: The Hallaton Treasure, a hoard of 5,000 silver and gold Iron Age coins of the Corieltavi tribe found near the village of Hallaton in south-east Leicestershire.

Right: Part of a clay tray used to melt metal in order to create blanks for making coins.

Left: The people of Iron Age Leicestershire were primarily farmers, most of them living as extended family groups in settlements scattered across the landscape.

Bottom Right: Iron Age Leicester as it may have looked from the south during the early 1st century AD. Artwork by Sarah Geeves.

Prehistoric Leicester (*Ratae*)
(mid 1st century BC to mid 1st century AD)

Speculation about Leicester's origins can be traced as far back as the early 12th century. In Geoffrey of Monmouth's part-historical, part-mythical chronicle of British history, the *Historia Regum Britanniae,* he attributes *Kaerleir* or *Leircestre*'s foundation to King Leir (later of Shakespearian fame) in *c.* 800 BC. This is of course fanciful and archaeological excavations over the last 75 years have firmly established that the first permanent settlement of Leicester occurred a little over 2000 years ago, during the 1st century BC.

The pre-Roman settlement of Leicester was the southern centre of the *Corieltavi*, a loose federation of tribal groups which controlled much of Leicestershire, Rutland, Lincolnshire and parts of Derbyshire, Nottinghamshire and Northamptonshire during the late Iron Age. The Romans later record its name as *Ratae*, a Celtic name meaning 'ramparts'. Evidence from Leicestershire suggests that the *Corieltavi* lived a largely rural life (**far left**) in farms and small village-like settlements. *Ratae* only developed at the end of the Iron Age, but quickly established extensive contacts with the rest of Britain and the Continent.

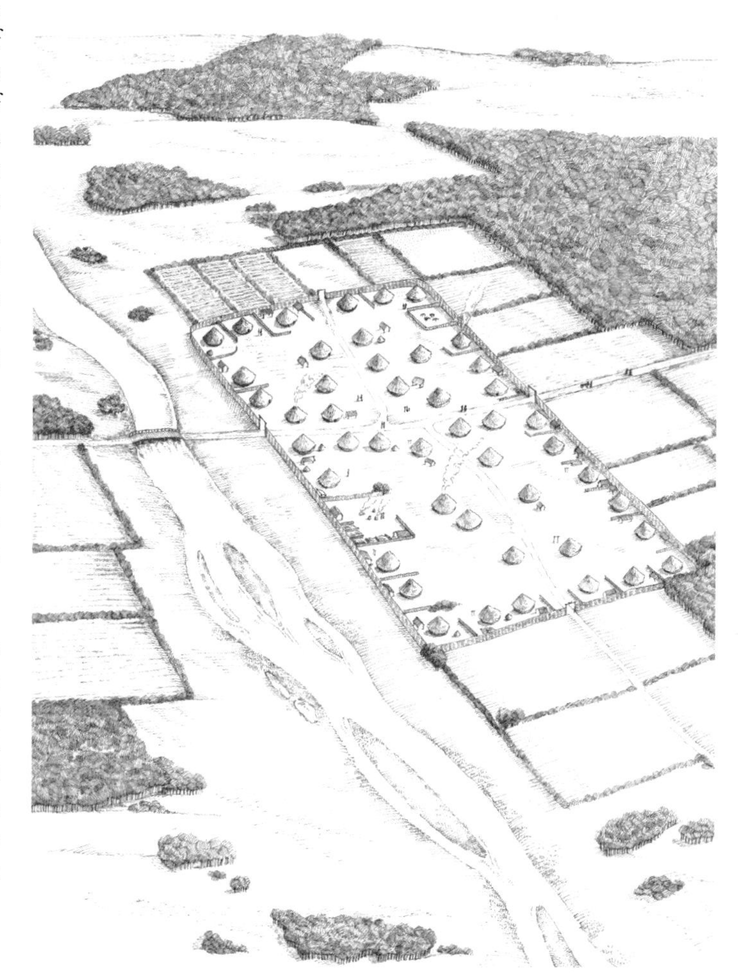

The first settlement (**right**) is thought to have been sited over a ten hectare area on the east bank of the River Soar near St Nicholas Circle in the modern city. The physical evidence largely consists of traces of roundhouses, pits, ditches and gullies, but the presence of high quality pottery and jewellery imported from Gaul (France), Italy and Spain together with tribal coins (**top left**) indicates that *Ratae* was a significant settlement of high status.

Another indication of *Ratae*'s importance is evidence for Iron Age coin production. This comes in the form of pieces of the clay trays (**above**) used to create coin blanks. Known as 'flan trays' these contain rows of small circular impressions of varying sizes, presumably representing different denominations of coin. Carefully measured portions of metal would have been placed in the holes, and the tray placed in a furnace for melting. The small globular pellets produced would then be hammered to a flat shape, and finally struck between two dies to produce the finished coin. Trays have been recovered from Bath Lane and show that the settlement was important enough to have a mint from the late 1st century BC.

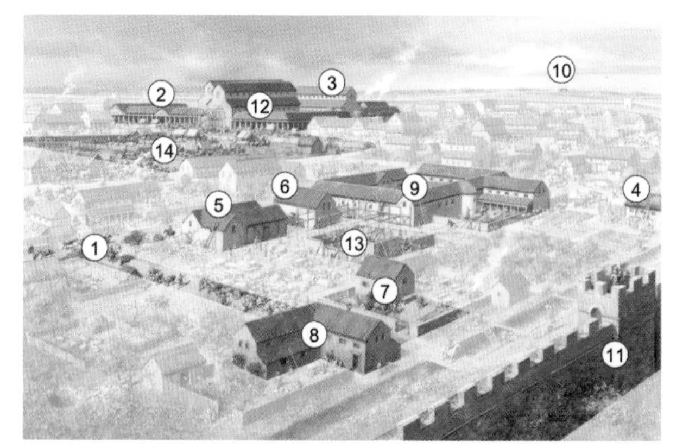

Roman Leicester (*Ratae Corieltavorum*)

(mid 1st to early 5th century AD)

In the years immediately following the Roman Conquest of Britain in AD 43, we suspect that a fort or fortress housing a military garrison was established at Leicester, although the archaeological evidence remains unclear. Roman occupation of *Ratae* seems to have developed initially as a continuation of the existing native settlement and on several excavations the remains of timber buildings and streets of the period have been found. These were on a variety of different alignments making it very difficult to see if there was any systematic layout to the early settlement.

By the early 2nd century AD the town had been reorganised and a new rectangular street grid, with drainage ditches and cambered gravel roads (**1**), was laid out. This probably coincided with *Ratae*'s appointment as the *civitas* capital of the *Corieltavi* tribe. From this moment new and increasingly sophisticated buildings begin to line the new streets and from the middle of the 2nd century major programmes of public and private building were undertaken in the town. Some examples have been found beneath the later town defences pointing to the rapid expansion of the settlement at this time. Public buildings included the *forum* and *basilica* (**2**), the Jewry Wall Public Baths (**3**) and at least one temple identified as a *Mithraeum* (dedicated to the Persian god Mithras), whilst private buildings included a variety of domestic, commercial and industrial premises. Masonry buildings were beginning to appear from the mid 2nd century. Some were perhaps commercial properties (**4–5**) or small houses (**6–8**), whilst others were palatial townhouses, of which the Vine Street Courtyard House is a fine example (**9**). Life was not restricted to the town, however: large suburbs grew up, whilst substantial villas such as the one found at Norfolk Street (**10**) were built in the surrounding countryside.

In the late 2nd century or early 3rd century, the town was provided with defences. At first these were simple ditches and earth ramparts but a substantial stone wall was added to the front of the rampart in the late 3rd century. A section of the town defences has been examined on Sanvey Gate where two large ditches were found in front of a 3m-wide wall and interval tower (**11**). The wall may have been about 4m high and would have been as much a symbol of civic pride as a discouragement to would-be invaders.

In this picture (**left**) Roman Leicester has reached the peak of its development. Commerce was booming by the late 3rd century and the town had established trading links across Britain and Western Europe. New building programmes saw the construction of a market-hall or *macellum* (**12**) north of the *forum* and other substantial commercial properties (**13**). Despite this, the evidence suggests that large areas inside the town remained undeveloped (**14**). These open spaces probably served as storage yards, market spaces and kitchen gardens.

What was happening in Leicester in the 4th century is less certain. This is largely because medieval cultivation and quarrying of Roman remains for building material has destroyed the evidence. One theory is that Leicester entered a prolonged period of decline from the mid 4th century onwards. This is typified by the deterioration of the prosperous courtyard house on Vine Street (**9**) into a row of workshops including a smithy.

Left: Roman Leicester (Ratae Corieltavorum) from the north-east, as it may have looked during the late 3rd century AD.

*Above: The Jewry Wall. Once part of a Roman public bath house (**3**), today this is one of the largest surviving fragments of a Roman building still standing in Britain.*

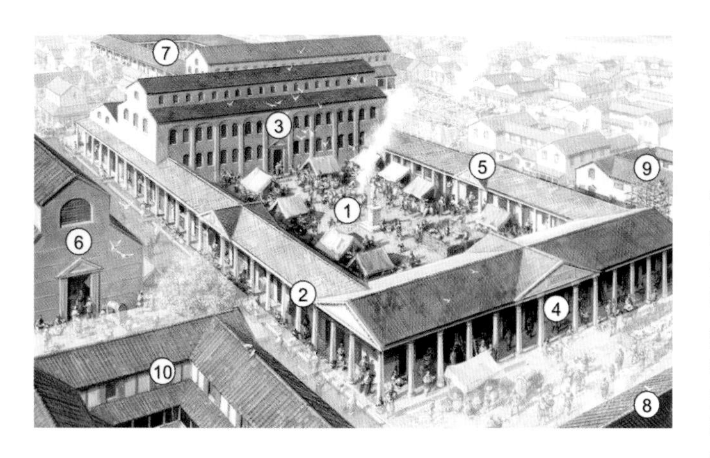

The Roman *Forum* and *Basilica*
(mid 2nd to 4th century AD)

When Leicester's street-grid was laid out in the early 2nd century AD, a large open area in the centre of the town appears to have been surfaced with gravel and set aside for the eventual construction of the main public buildings. These included the *forum* and *basilica* which functioned not only as a market-place but also as a centre for social, political and religious gatherings. Building the *forum* would have been a major undertaking in any Roman town, comparable to constructing a medieval cathedral, and it would have taken perhaps fifty or sixty years to complete. Leicester's adoption of the municipal trappings of urban life occurred much later than in many other Romano-British towns and the *forum* was probably not completed until the middle of the 2nd century AD.

The *forum* was a large open square (**1**) surrounded on three sides by colonnades containing shops (**2**) and enclosed on the fourth by the *basilica* (**3**), a large aisled building which housed offices and served as the town's administrative and judicial centre. The main pedestrian access to the *forum* would have been via the south range (**4**), whilst wheeled traffic was probably admitted via a wider entrance in the east range (**5**). On completion the entire complex would have measured some 130m by 90m – larger than many football pitches.

Despite some evidence from small excavations in the 1960s and 70s, we know very little about the *forum*'s internal appearance. It was evidently of high-quality construction, but most of the rooms were provided with plain clay or concrete floors, giving the impression of a very functional building. Some rooms were eventually redecorated with mosaic pavements and painted or marble-veneered walls and it is conceivable that traders were responsible for the upkeep and decoration of their own shops. Sadly, no direct evidence for the function of any of these shops has yet been discovered, but some had timber partitions which perhaps functioned as counters, whilst others contained small hearths which may have been for cooking food, providing warmth or for industrial purposes such as metalworking.

The area surrounding the *forum* contained a variety of public and private buildings. To the west was the Jewry Wall public bathhouse (**6**) and Leicester's only known Roman temple, a *Mithraeum*, whilst to the north commercial activity had expanded out of the *forum* into a *macellum* or market-hall (**7**). Evidence suggests the area surrounding the *forum* also contained smaller commercial and domestic properties. South of the *forum*, rows of timber shops initially lined the street (**8**); these were rebuilt in stone during the early 3rd century. To the east, further substantial stone buildings (**9**) have been uncovered beneath what is now the BBC building on St Nicholas Place, whilst to the west was a large mid 2nd-century townhouse (**10**), now beneath St Nicholas Circle. This house contained the Peacock pavement, one of the finest mosaic floors discovered in Roman Britain.

Little is known of the *forum*'s final years, but repairs and renovations seem to have continued into the 4th century AD. Although evidence for a fire was found, damage was perhaps comparatively minor, as a new floor was laid in one of the affected rooms some time after AD 364 (based on the discovery of a coin of this date from beneath it).

Left: The Roman Forum and Basilica as they may have looked from the south-west during the early 3rd century AD.

Right: The central panel of the 2nd-century Peacock Mosaic Pavement discovered in 1898 on St Nicholas Street, now part of St Nicholas Circle. It came from a Roman town house, partly excavated in 1968.

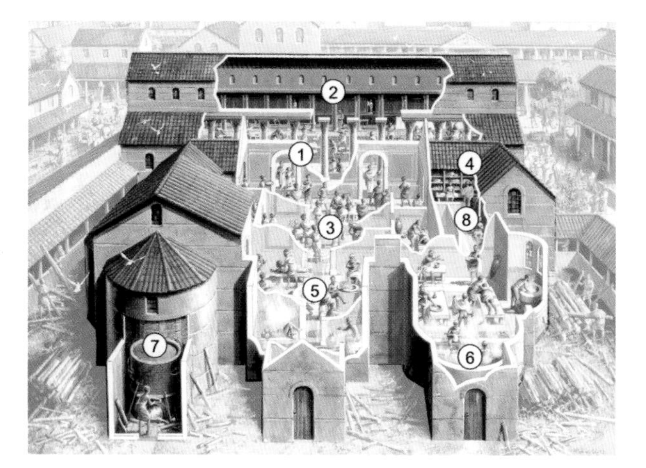

The Jewry Wall Roman Baths

(mid 2nd to 4th century AD)

Today, the only visible reminder of Leicester's Roman past is the Jewry Wall. At 23m long, 8m high and 2.5m thick, it is one of the largest pieces of Roman masonry still standing in Britain. Since the medieval period, when it was commonly believed to be part of a temple to Janus, there has been much discussion about what the Jewry Wall may have been. It was not until it was excavated in the late 1930s (**bottom right**) by the pioneering archaeologist Dame Kathleen Kenyon (coincidentally in preparation for the building of a new swimming baths) that its role as part of a substantial bathing complex was demonstrated. Kenyon's excavations were the first large-scale archaeological investigation of Roman Leicester and paved the way for seventy-five years of archaeological discoveries.

Bathing was an integral part of cultural and social life in Roman towns regardless of who you were. Bath-houses were not just places to get clean: customers would also exercise, relax, eat, socialise and conduct business. They would now be considered similar to community centres, combining all the facilities provided by gyms, spas, libraries, shopping centres and restaurants.

Built in the mid 2nd century AD, the bath complex did not change much and probably remained in use until the 4th century AD. Access to the baths is thought to have been through arches in the Jewry Wall (**1**). This was the west wall of a large, aisled *basilica* on the eastern side of the complex (**2**), most of which now lies beneath the church of St Nicholas. This was the *palaestra*, the exercise hall where men could meet, box, wrestle and play ball games. The central focus of the baths themselves was the *tepidarium* (**3**), the warm room heated from under the floor through a hypocaust, where bathers could assemble and relax before moving on to the warm or cold baths. Here they would cover themselves with oils and use a tool called a strigil to scrape off the dirt and oil. On each side of the *tepidarium* was an *apodyterium* (**4**), a changing-room with latrines where belongings would be looked after by personal or hired slaves. The three hot rooms or *caldaria* (**5**) were situated on the western side of the complex and would have been maintained at a temperature of about 40° C. They contained pools of hot water (**6**) which was heated in tanks over furnaces fuelled from external stoke-rooms (**7**). This would have made the rooms very humid, much like a modern sauna. The final step was to plunge into a pool of cold water in the *frigidarium* (**8**), to close the pores and refresh the body.

Left: A cut-away impression of how the Jewry Wall baths may have looked during the late 2nd century AD.

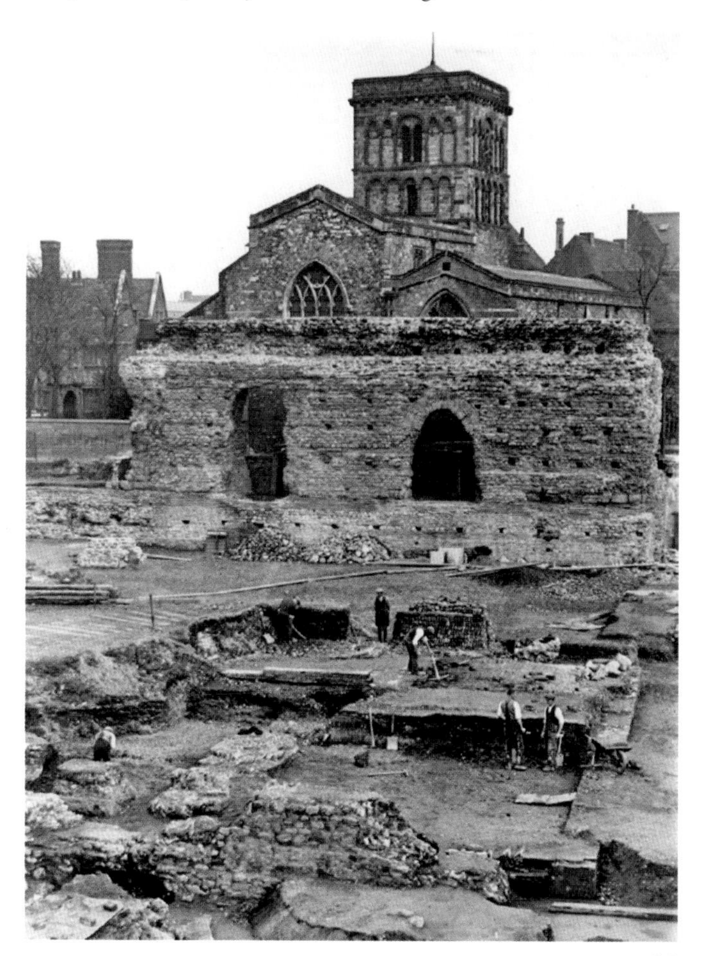

Right: The excavation of the Jewry Wall Roman baths in the late 1930s. Photograph courtesy of Leicester Arts and Museums Service.

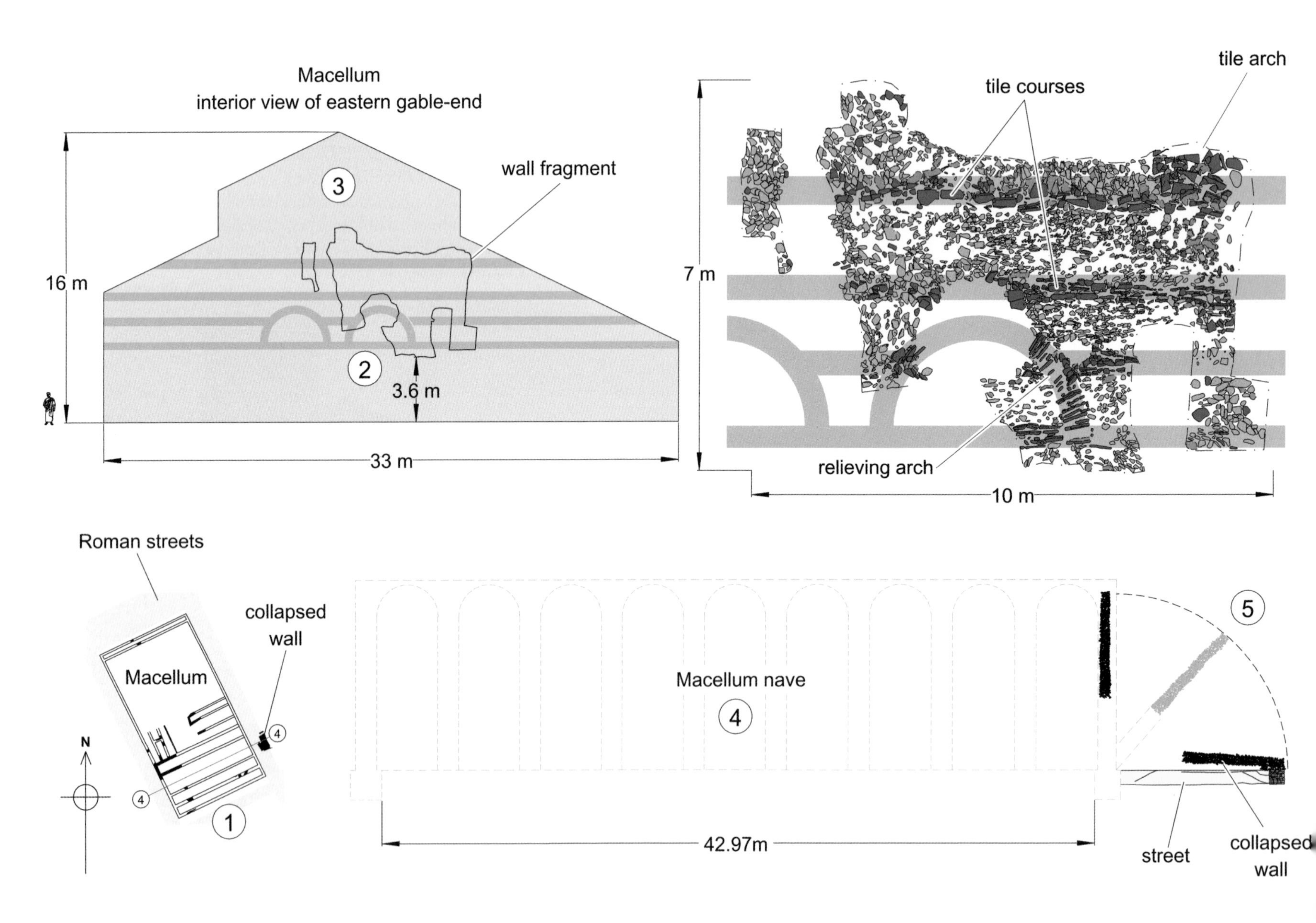
Macellum
interior view of eastern gable-end
wall fragment
3
2
16 m
3.6 m
33 m
tile arch
tile courses
7 m
relieving arch
10 m
Roman streets
collapsed
wall
Macellum
N
4
4
1
Macellum nave
4
5
42.97m
street
collapsed
wall

The Roman Market-Hall (*Macellum*)
(early 3rd century to 5th century AD)

A sign of Leicester's increasing prosperity during the Roman period can be seen in the construction of what we believe to be a market-hall or *macellum*, north of the *forum* during the early 3rd century AD. Built on similar lines, this too had a colonnaded square alongside a large hall, but would have been solely devoted to commerce. First discovered in 1958, today it lies beneath the Travelodge on Highcross Street, and excavations have shown that the main hall was orientated east to west with a central nave flanked by aisles (**1**). The hall was simply floored with durable concrete but its walls and ceilings were lavishly decorated with painted plaster. The *macellum* would have been full of small shops and market stalls set up in the aisles and between the colonnades – rather like Leicester Market today.

A remarkable archaeological discovery was made in 2006 on the east side of Highcross Street (**below**). An extensive horizontal spread of stone and tile rubble turned out to be the collapsed eastern gable-end wall of the *macellum*. The area of masonry measured at least 7m by 10m and it was built in a similar manner to the Jewry Wall, with granite rubble separated by bands of red terracotta tiles. Based on the projected width of the Roman street next to the *macellum*, we suspect that the base of its east wall lay beneath the middle of present-day Highcross Street. If correct, this would suggest that the fallen wall broke off at a level of about 3.6m above the ground (**2**). This means that archaeologists can now visualise how this end of the building may have looked (**3**), and it has been calculated that it would have been at least 16m in height. That is equivalent to a three- or four-storey building today.

The collapsed wall also included two tile arches. At the bottom of the surviving fragment was part of what is known as a 'relieving arch' incorporated into the wall to help distribute its weight evenly, possibly over a window. Near the top was the beginning of an arch springing from the wall at right-angles. This shows that the nave and aisles in the *macellum* were separated by an arched colonnade (**4**).

The *macellum* probably fell out of use during the late 4th century AD. Eventually, large panels of plaster fell from the ceiling and were left uncleared across the floor, and soil accumulated inside the building suggesting that a prolonged period of neglect had set in. Parts of the building seem to have been destroyed more dramatically in a large fire.

The gable wall finally collapsed during the second half of the 5th century AD (**5**). Prior to this, it had lost most of its facing stones and exposure to weathering would have weakened it further, making its collapse inevitable.

Left: Reconstructions showing how the east wall of the macellum is thought to have collapsed across the adjacent Roman street.

Right: The excavation of the collapsed wall on Highcross Street in 2006. Beneath it were the remains of an earlier Roman wall and street, and a small group of furnaces.

Left: The entrance to the Roman forum as it may have looked during the 2nd and 3rd century AD.

Below: A small beaker or cup of the sort used to drink wine. Its style indicates that it was made sometime between AD 120 and AD 160. Reproduced at actual size.

Top right: Fresh meat and vegetables on sale in a Roman shop.

Right: Broken pottery found in a refuse pit behind a row of Roman shops near St Nicholas Circle. This group of material was unusual because it mostly contained amphorae, bowls, jars and flagons but no drinking vessels, plates or mixing dishes such as mortaria. This suggests food was not being consumed on the premises, so the shop was perhaps a delicatessen rather than a tavern. The amphorae would have been used to transport olive oil, wine, fruits and preserves from the continent; the bowls to display food; and the jars and flagons to decant products for sale.

Bottom right: A Roman steelyard found on Vine Street. A steelyard was a type of balance used to weigh small items of merchandise. Reproduced at actual size.

Living in Roman Leicester

Recent excavations have shed new light on everyday life in Roman Leicester. The most common finds were sherds of broken pottery. Pottery was mass-produced in the Roman period making it a cheap, hard-wearing alternative to glass and metal, which could easily be replaced if broken. The inhabitants of Leicester used pottery from Cambridgeshire, Warwickshire and Dorset as well as wares imported from Spain, Gaul (France), Germany, Italy and North Africa. A wide variety of vessels was available, from fine table wares for serving food and drink to more utilitarian pots for cooking and storage. All would have been readily available to buy in shops and stalls in the *forum*, the *macellum* or elsewhere in the town. Food too was imported in large quantities, with olive oil, wine and fish sauce all brought by sea from the continent in large storage vessels called amphorae.

Food remains found in Leicester show that people enjoyed a varied diet. Barley and spelt wheat, which were used to make bread and porridge and to thicken stews, were cultivated locally, as were peas, beans, leaf beets, apples, plums and cherries. Wild foods were also harvested, including hazelnuts, sloes, blackberries, elder and sorrel. Most people could season dishes with wild mint, coriander, opium poppy and mustard, whilst the rich could afford imported foods such as lentils and dried fruit. Meat mostly came from domesticated cattle, sheep, goat, pig and fowl, but wild deer, hare, geese, duck, woodcock and coot were also hunted. The fish that were consumed were mainly eels and herrings, together with freshwater varieties caught locally. Oysters too were a common food and were probably transported from the Essex coast. Finds of shell indicate that eggs were eaten, whilst other foods which must have been consumed, such as honey, milk, and cheese, have left no trace. Although most food was sold in the *forum* and the market-hall, a recent excavation on Castle Street has revealed evidence for a Roman 'delicatessen' selling both local foodstuffs and exotic imports, such as figs, grapes and olives.

Roman Leicester would have been a bustling place full of opportunities to work and to shop. Unfortunately – with the exception of the possible delicatessen – it has not yet been possible to discover what was sold in specific shops; nevertheless, people in Leicester owned a vast array of personal items including jewellery, tweezers and mirrors, and everyday household items such as knives, spoons and *styli* for writing. Some of these were of continental manufacture but most were locally produced. Further evidence for commerce is apparent in the number of steelyard beams (weighing apparatus) found during recent excavations (see page 31), whilst recreational items included bone dice and large numbers of gaming counters. Most of these are found by archaeologists because they had become lost or broken and thrown away and they show that the people of Roman Leicester were as diverse and multicultural in their tastes as the city's inhabitants are today.

Abundant evidence of craft activities has been found – although organic materials such as wood and textiles rarely survive, the tools used to work them frequently do. Iron, bronze, lead, glass, bone, horn and leather were all being worked in Leicester and examples of such manufacture include bone pin workshops and a smithy found at Vine Street (see page 35).

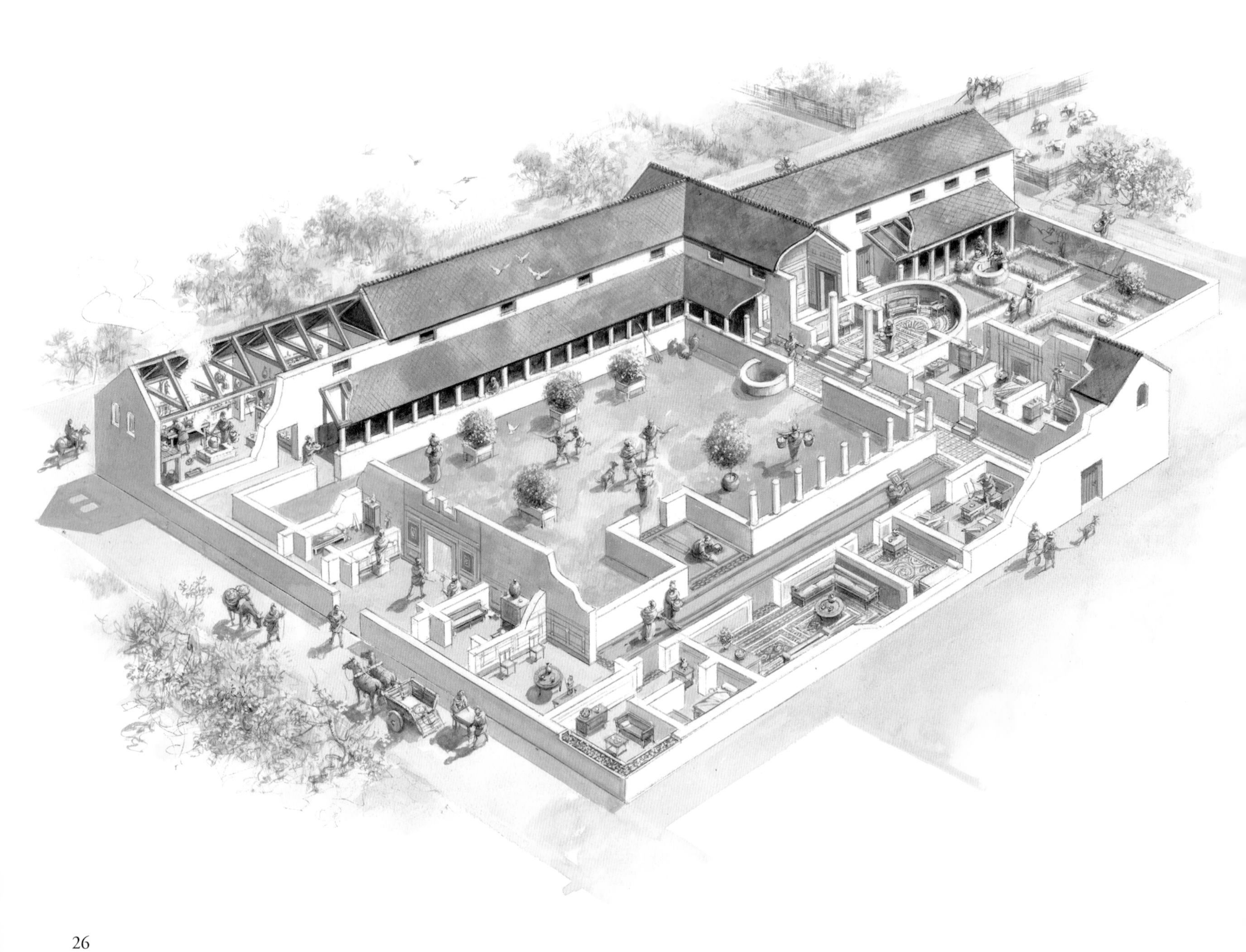

Roman Townhouses

As well as Leicester's Roman public buildings, archaeologists have also uncovered a number of private houses. These ranged from rows of small, simple rectangular buildings, to large, elaborate Mediterranean-style houses. Whilst public buildings were normally constructed in stone, houses and many of the other privately owned buildings were built using dried clay bricks, timber, or a combination of the two. Stone was used in some homes, however, including the Vine Street Courtyard House (**left**). Roofs were either thatched, in the case of the poorer buildings, or covered with slate or tiles. Ceramic tiles were laid out on the ground to dry before they were fired and it seems children, cats, dogs and sheep were all allowed to roam freely across them, often leaving impressions of their feet. The courtyard house on Vine Street was roofed with diamond-shaped stone slates (**1**), quarried locally near Groby. When the building was demolished in the late 4th century these were carefully recovered from the roof and stacked in the courtyard for intended re-use.

Most floors would have been made of compacted earth but in some houses concrete floors were laid in the more important rooms or were decorated with mosaic pavements (**2**). Walls and ceilings were rendered with plaster and painted with a variety of effects (**3**), including imitation marbling, geometric panels, architectural friezes, figures and foliage. Little painted wall-plaster has been found in-situ during recent excavations but in the late 1950s a large house, now beneath Vaughan Way, was partially excavated. Known as the Blue Boar Lane townhouse this was built in the early 2nd century AD and was occupied for around 40 years before it was demolished to make way for the *macellum*. Two ranges of rooms were found surrounding a colonnaded courtyard. These were all floored with concrete or mosaic pavements and the walls were decorated with elaborate architectural and figurative schemes.

Until recently this was the largest Roman townhouse excavated in Leicester, but it has now been surpassed in size by the Vine Street courtyard house. This spacious home measured 40m by 40m and, with four ranges of rooms linked by corridors surrounding a central courtyard, it would have been an ostentatious display of wealth. The main reception and formal dining rooms (**4**) were positioned facing the entrance (**5**). These would probably have been reserved for special occasions and other large reception rooms (**6**) would have been used on an everyday basis. In one corner of the building was a kitchen (**7**), whilst a range of smaller rooms would have acted as more private sitting rooms, bedrooms, offices and porter's lodges. The large courtyard could be viewed from all sides and contained an ornamental pool (**8**) and land behind the building may have been laid out as a formal garden (**9**).

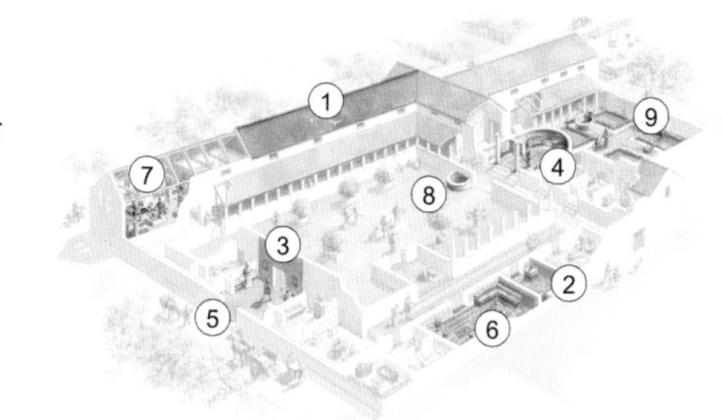

Far left: A view inside the courtyard house on Vine Street as it may have looked during the late 3rd century AD.

Above: Archaeologist John Wacher records the remains of the Blue Boar Lane townhouse in 1958. Clay-brick walls survived to nearly a metre high above the floor and were still decorated with painted plaster.

Left: Fragment of a tessellated pavement uncovered in a corridor of the Vine Street courtyard house.

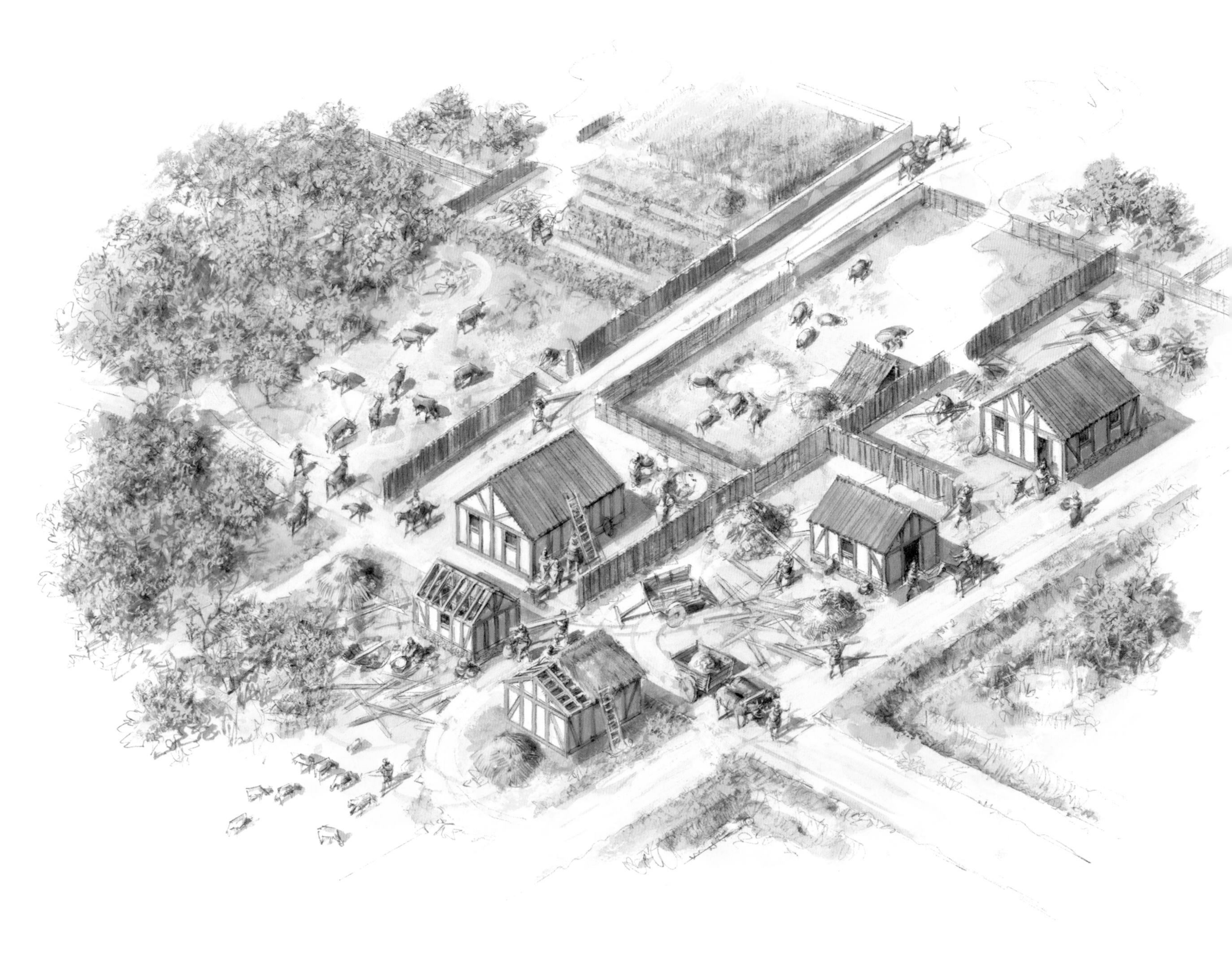

The Timber Buildings at Vine Street
(early to mid 2nd century AD)

These timber buildings were the first to occupy blocks of land, known as *insulae* ('islands'), created by the regular grid of streets established in the north-east part of the town in the early 2nd century AD.

Three buildings were identified in the corner of one *insula* during the excavation on Vine Street (**1-3**). The walls were probably timber-framed, resting on low stone walls with substantial footings. All the buildings were surrounded by gravel yards, whilst to the rear were small fields and stock pens extending into the interior of the *insula*. Fences surrounded the buildings and fields, and their positions could still be traced through lines of holes left behind when the posts were removed. Part of an iron ox goad (a long, metal-tipped pole used to guide livestock, particularly oxen pulling a plough) found in one of these post-holes further supports an agricultural use of the land and suggests the boundary between urban and rural life was quite fluid at this time.

Scientific analysis of the soil from the area behind the buildings (**4**) showed that it was mixed with pig slurry, an indication that these smallholdings were given over to rearing pigs. Animal bones recovered from hearths in the two larger buildings shows that the occupants of one (**1**) were eating domesticated animals including cattle, sheep, pig and fowl, whilst those in the other (**2**) were consuming more wild foods including deer and hazelnuts.

Further occupation was also identified in a neighbouring *insula* (**5**). Here there was a fourth building, but all that survived was a hearth and parts of a compacted earth floor. The hearth produced burnt food (peas and beans), whilst lying next to it was part of a small quernstone which would have been used to grind flour.

Only fifty years after the street-grid was laid out, these buildings were falling into decline and being replaced by larger, longer-lasting structures. This initial occupation probably originated as a rapid reaction to the emerging economic prospects brought on by Leicester's establishment as a *civitas* (tribal capital) but gave way to more permanent buildings once the town's future was assured.

Left: Looking across Vine Street from the south as it may have been during the early to mid-2nd century AD.

Above and below: A 2nd-century brooch (above) and a bronze hairpin (below). Both had been lost in the yards behind buildings 1, 2 and 3. Reproduced at actual size.

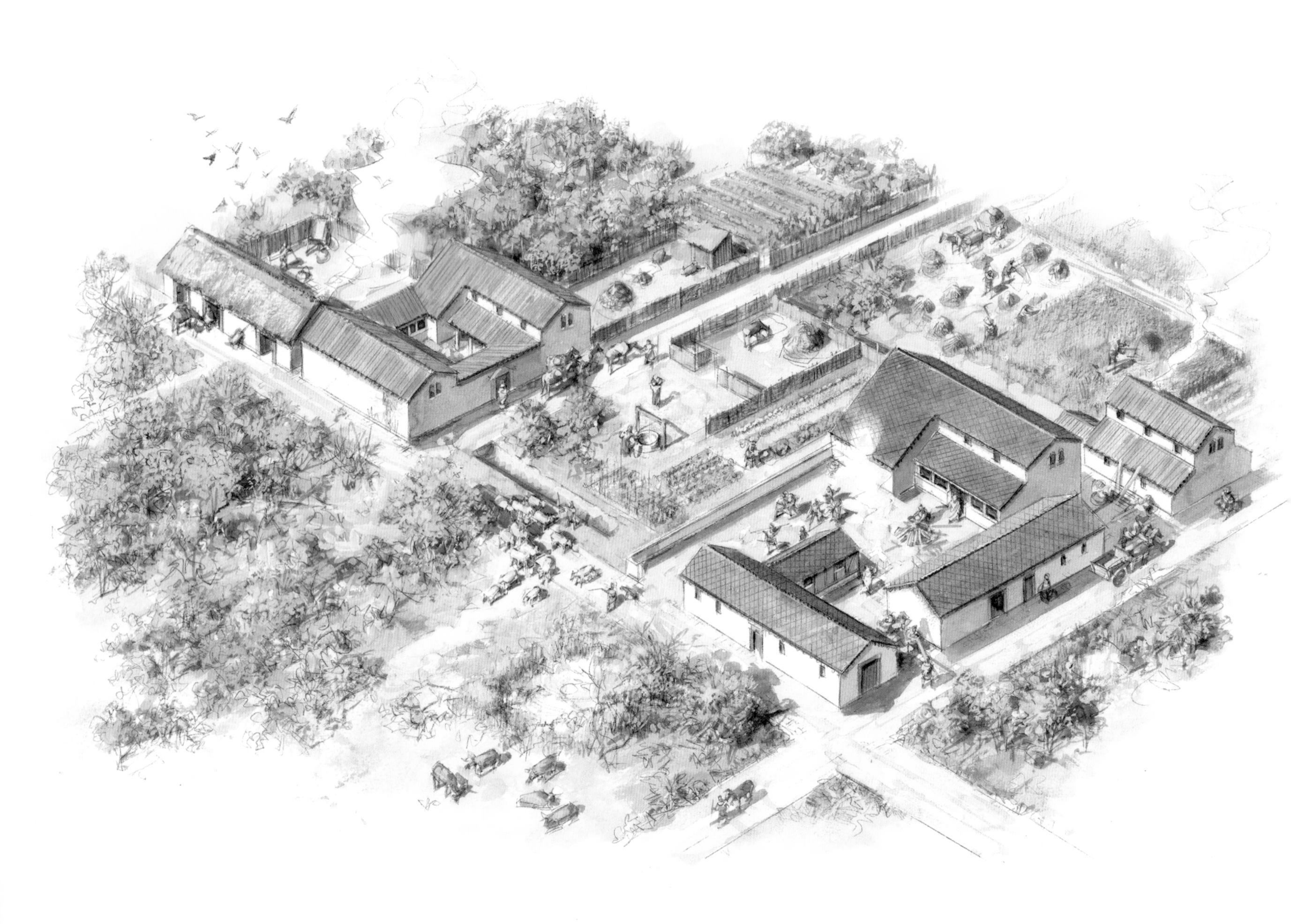

The Early Masonry Buildings at Vine Street
(mid to late 2nd century AD)

By the late 2nd century AD, the timber buildings had been replaced with more permanent masonry structures. These appeared to have been a mixture of workshops and private dwellings situated in an area of the town still predominantly used for cultivation. One house was modelled on a Mediterranean design (**1**) and was built around a central courtyard, whilst another contained a small private bath-suite with a room and a pool (**2**) heated from under the floor through a hypocaust. Work on this seems never to have been finished and the project was probably abandoned shortly after the rest of the house was completed. In fact, subsidence seems to have caused serious structural problems in this house, leading to continual renovation, and it may never have been built as intended. By the late 2nd century it had been turned into a small workshop making bone pins and needles. Waste from this manufacture was found in nearby pits along with a steelyard, a balance used to weigh items (see page 25). Unfortunately, little can be said about the Mediterranean-style house (**1**) as it was thoroughly demolished during the Roman period and all that remained was the outline of the wall footings and small patches of floor.

Three slate-roofed buildings near the street-junction may have formed a single property containing a house and associated workshops. Traces of metalworking were found around both workshops (**3**) and in the thatched building to the far left (**4**). Waste slag and crucible fragments show that both copper and iron were being melted and worked but sadly no sign of what the metals were being turned into was found. The workshops had access directly onto the street, whereas the house (**5**) was entered from a yard to the rear of the other buildings.

The large slate-roofed house (**5**) was the home of a prosperous family. Its interior was decorated with large vivid panels of painted wall plaster, some imitating expensive marble wall veneers and making use of costly imported pigments to colour the paint. Broken glass from the surrounding yards suggests that the windows were glazed, whilst two keys found during the excavation (**right**) indicate that the doors were secured by locks.

The house's occupants were also affluent enough to afford luxury foods such as grapes and to own a diverse range of personal possessions, some of which were lost over time in the surrounding yards. These items included coins, brooches, bracelets, pins, gaming counters, a spoon (**right**) and spindle whorls which demonstrate that a variety of domestic and leisure pursuits were taking place alongside the manufacturing activities of the neighbouring workshops.

By the end of the century, however, the three slate-roofed buildings (**3** and **5**) had fallen on hard times and were in a neglected, semi-derelict state with soil accumulating in some of the rooms and others being used as latrines. Hay was present in the house (**5**) and it may have been used to store animal fodder.

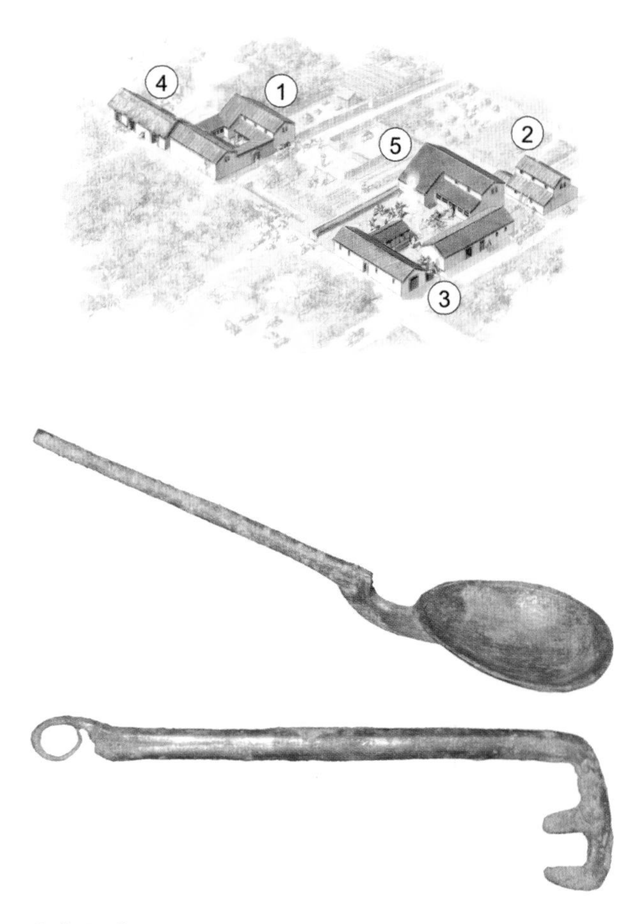

Left: Looking across Vine Street from the south as it may have been during the mid to late 2nd century AD.

*Above: A Roman bronze spoon of a design common from the 2nd century onwards. The end of its handle has broken off and it had been dropped or thrown out in the yard next to the slate-roofed house (**5**). Reproduced at actual size.*

*Above: An L-shaped Roman key or latch-lifter. This was a primitive form of key which would have been pushed through a hole in a door to fit into a latch to lift and move it. It was found in the yard behind the workshops (**3**). Reproduced at actual size.*

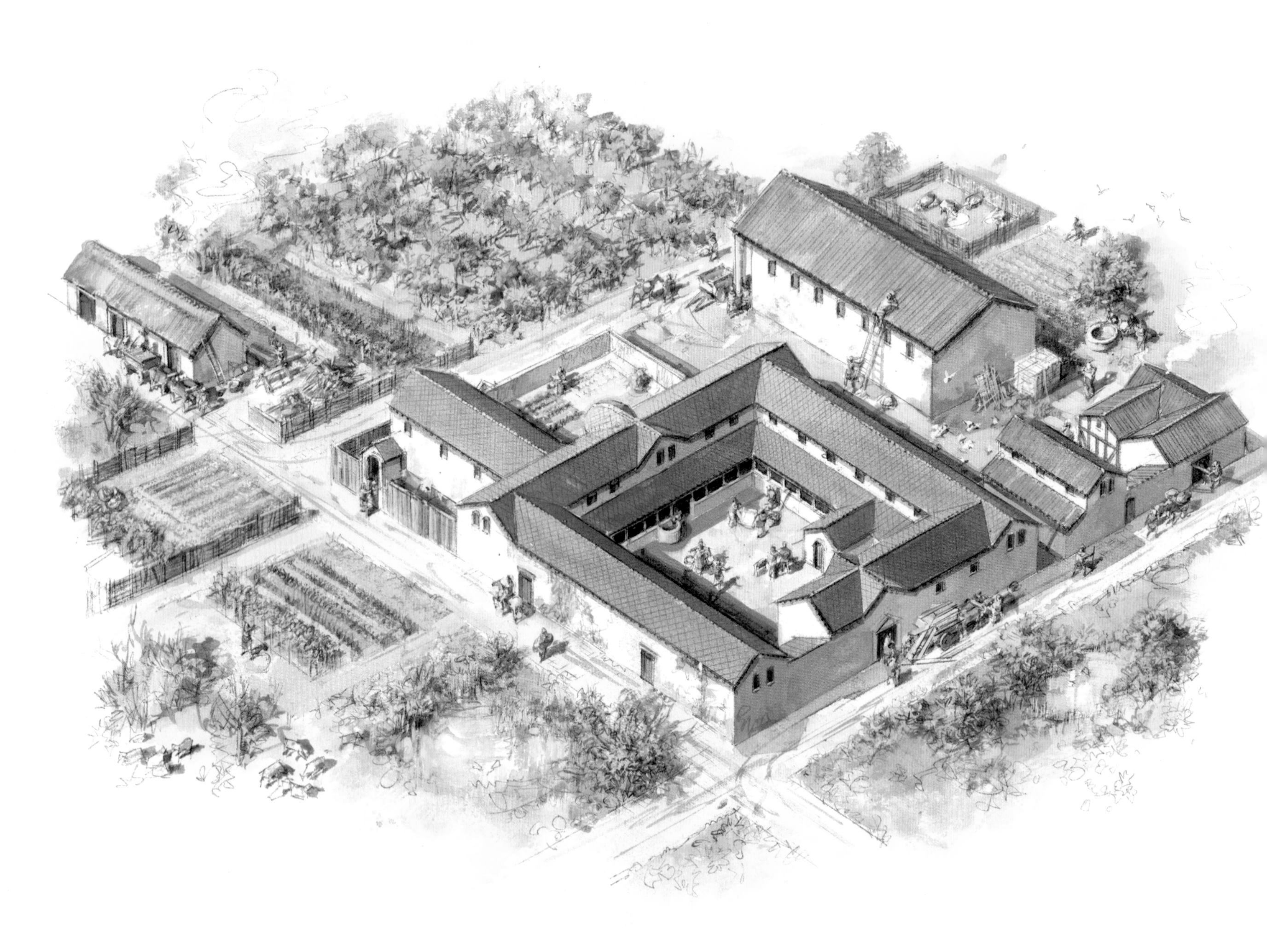

The Vine Street Courtyard House
(early 3rd to mid 4th century AD)

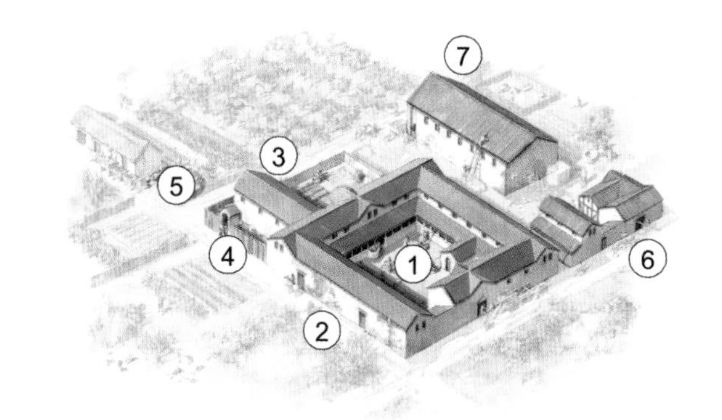

During the early 3rd century, the south-west corner of the *insula* experienced major redevelopment and the semi-derelict buildings were incorporated into a substantial courtyard house (**1**). The central courtyard was enclosed by a corridor providing access to suites of rooms in the four ranges. In all, the house contained at least twenty-six rooms. Most of these were furnished with concrete floors and elaborately painted walls and some were heated from under the floor through hypocausts. In the western range (**2**) the rooms were more utilitarian and may have been related to the running of the house. One of them was almost certainly a kitchen as suggested by the remains of foodstuffs found from its floor. By the early 4th century, another wing had been added to the rear of the house (**3**) and many of the rooms in the original house had been decorated with mosaics. The rooms in the new wing were also provided with under-floor heating, the furnace for which was located in a small yard fenced off from the street (**4**). On the opposite side of the new wing a veranda opened out onto an enclosed garden behind the house.

Finds from two late 3rd-century waste pits to the rear produced an extraordinary quantity of evidence for the lifestyle of its occupants. In addition to staple foods such as wheat, their diet included a wide variety of local fruits, fish and meat. Game was also served at table and the occupants could afford imported fruits such as figs, sea fish and oysters. At one meal, a large freshwater fish known as a barbel, which was nearly half a metre in length, had been served. Holes through some of the cattle bones suggest that the beef was hung up to smoke or cure.

Food and drink was stored and prepared in a wide range of bowls and jars including amphorae and *mortaria* (mixing bowls), before being served in fine quality glass and pottery vessels and dishes. Many of the broken cooking pots still showed evidence of sooting on their exterior and limescale or food remains on their interior. The occupants kept dogs, although whether they were pets or guard or hunting dogs is not known. They also owned a wide variety of personal possessions, some of which had become lost or discarded in the waste pits. These included coins, gaming counters and an elaborate key handle (**right**). These finds, together with the size and decoration of the courtyard house all indicate that it was the home of a wealthy household, with a rich family served by a large number of servants and slaves.

The 3rd century also saw the disappearance of the small Mediterranean-style courtyard house and the expansion of the small aisled house (**6**) into a sprawling collection of buildings extending along the street. By the early 4th century a large building had been erected away from the streets, behind the other buildings (**7**). This was of substantial construction with massive stone walls supporting a very wide roof. Its northern end may have had a portico, suggesting this was the entrance, which was accessed from an alleyway running behind the courtyard house. Inside it was very simple with only two plain rooms. Although we cannot be certain, this building may have had a commercial purpose, possibly a large warehouse.

Left: Looking across Vine Street from the south as it may have been during the early 4th century AD (for an interior view of the courtyard house see page 26).

*Above: An elaborate 3rd-century key handle. This was found in a large refuse pit next to the courtyard house (**1**). The key itself was not found and it may have been broken and then thrown away rather than being accidentally dropped and lost in the pit. Reproduced at actual size.*

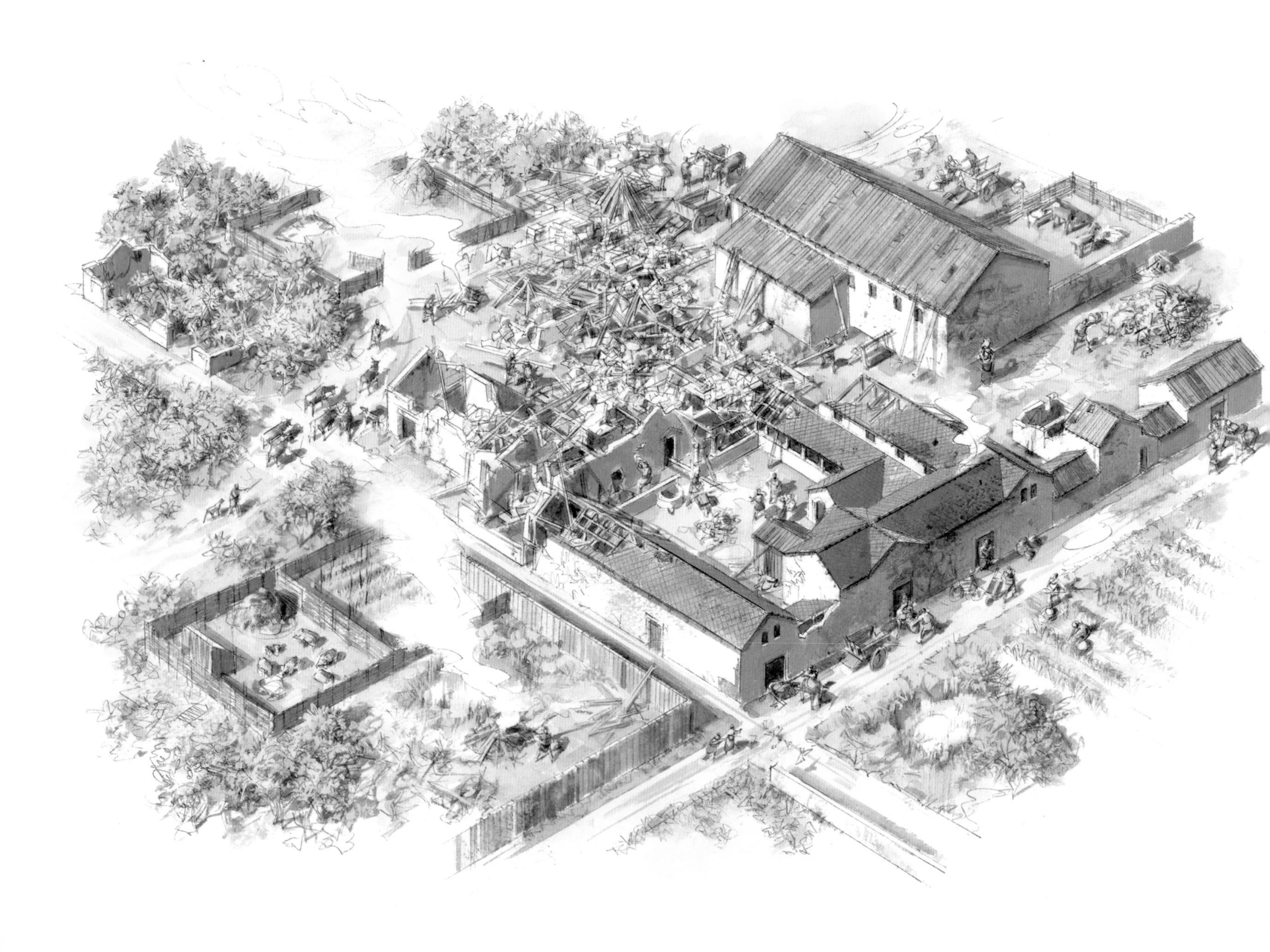

The Final Masonry Buildings at Vine Street
(mid to late 4th century AD)

By the mid 4th century, domestic habitation in the area was beginning to decline. The large courtyard house, having been lived in for 150 years or more, ceased to be inhabited by a wealthy family and its northern ranges were deliberately demolished (**1**). This may have been done with the intention of re-using any reclaimed building material elsewhere in town, as stacks of salvaged roof slates and piles of tesserae recovered from mosaics were found amongst the debris.

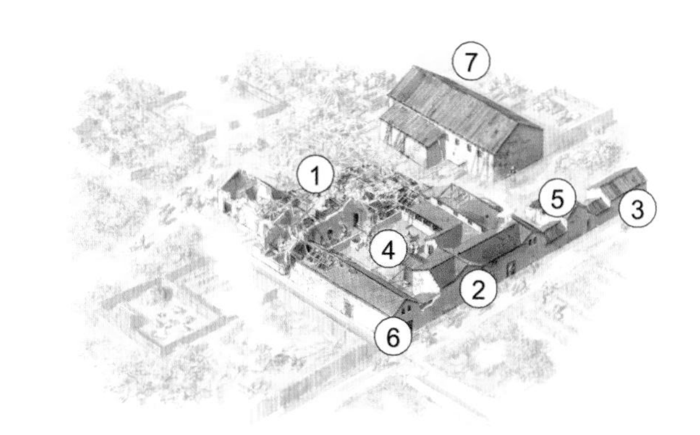

The southern range (**2**) and the small aisled house to the east (**3**) were merged to become a series of small workshops, and a number of timber lean-to structures were built in the area which had once been the main courtyard (**4**). Bone and metalworking took place in the workshops, with at least one room (**5**) being used to manufacture bone pins and needles and another being used as a smithy (**6**). Another room may have served either as an animal byre or an open latrine as it was filled with effluent.

The smithy was the final activity in the room next to the junction of the streets and archaeologists found that the floor was still covered with thick deposits of charcoal and hammerscale (the minute, molten 'sparks' produced when hammering red-hot metal). Forensic analysis of the hammerscale identified a radiating pattern decreasing in density away from a single focal point, which positioned the anvil near the centre of the room. Several broken metal tools were also found amongst the smithing waste.

Signs of a breakdown in social order were found in the ruins of the courtyard house in the form of deliberately hidden valuables. One cache contained a very large ingot of recycled lead (requiring several people to lift it) which had been carefully concealed in a hole beneath the floor. It was found undisturbed, showing that no-one had returned to reclaim the lead. In another room, a hoard of 542 coins was found in another hole. The coins all dated to between AD 320 and 335 and although they may originally have been buried in a wooden chest, they seem to have been disturbed in the late 360s or 370s, based on the discovery of a single later coin of the Emperor Valens (AD 364–378) in the same deposit. One possible explanation is that the coins were buried as part of a much larger cache of valuables which were subsequently stolen or recovered by their owner. The coins, however, were made mainly of copper with a tiny amount of silver and their low intrinsic value may explain why they were thrown back in the hole.

In contrast, the large building to the rear of the street frontage prospered and was even enlarged (**7**), with new rooms and a walled yard added in the 4th century. Numerous late Roman coins, including some dating to the very late 4th century, were recovered from the vicinity. This suggests that the building was still being used towards the end of, and possibly after, the official Roman government of Britain ended in AD 410.

Far left: Looking across Vine Street from the south as it may have been during the mid 4th century AD.

Above: Part of the coin hoard, which was found in discrete groups of coins, heaped as if they were spilling out of a chest which had been tipped on its side.

Left: One of the commonest coins in the hoard, a copper-alloy coin minted in London in AD 323–324 for the Emperor Constantine I. On one side the Emperor's head is depicted. On the other side is an altar surrounded by the inscription BEATA TRANQVILLITAS meaning 'Blessed Tranquillity'. Reproduced at actual size.

The Vine Street Curse Tablets

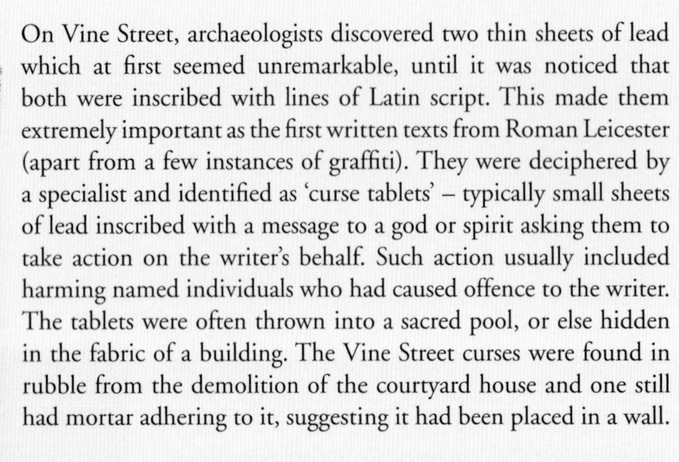

On Vine Street, archaeologists discovered two thin sheets of lead which at first seemed unremarkable, until it was noticed that both were inscribed with lines of Latin script. This made them extremely important as the first written texts from Roman Leicester (apart from a few instances of graffiti). They were deciphered by a specialist and identified as 'curse tablets' – typically small sheets of lead inscribed with a message to a god or spirit asking them to take action on the writer's behalf. Such action usually included harming named individuals who had caused offence to the writer. The tablets were often thrown into a sacred pool, or else hidden in the fabric of a building. The Vine Street curses were found in rubble from the demolition of the courtyard house and one still had mortar adhering to it, suggesting it had been placed in a wall.

Today, such curses are important because they reveal something of the voices of ordinary people which would otherwise be totally lost. Around 500 tablets have been discovered across the Roman Empire of which over half come from Britain, mostly from the sacred springs at Bath in Somerset and at a shrine at Uley in Gloucestershire. To come across them elsewhere is unusual and the two from Vine Street are the first to be found in Leicester.

The Vine Street tablets bear a style of script which was commonly used for everyday documents and letters and the style of language suggests they were written between AD 150 and AD 250. The first, the Servandus Tablet (named after its writer) refers to a Celtic god, Maglus and lists the names of 19 suspects of a theft, thought to be household slaves from the courtyard house (see page 33). The Sabinianus Tablet mentions a *septisonium,* which is believed to be a form of monumental façade depicting the seven gods after whom the Roman days of the week were named (the Sun and Moon, Mars, Mercury, Jupiter, Venus, and Saturn). It is only the fourth known reference to such a structure in the Roman Empire.

The Servandus Tablet (left)
Measures 201mm by 78mm

'I give to the god Maglus him who did wrong from the slave-quarters; I give him who did theft the cloak from the slave-quarters; who stole the cloak of Servandus: Silvester, Rigomandus, Senilis, Venustinus, Vorvena, Calaminus, Felicianus, Rufaedo, Vendicina, Ingenuinus, Iuventius, Alocus, Cennosus, Germanus, Senedo, Cunovendus, Regalis, Nigella, Senicianus [*deleted*]. I give that the god Maglus before the ninth day take away him who stole the cloak of Servandus.'

The Sabinianus Tablet (detail below)
Measures 123mm by 69mm

'Those who have stolen the silver coins of Sabinianus, that is Similis, Cupitus, Lochita, a god will strike down in this *septisonium*, and I ask that they lose their life before seven days.

Depictions of Gods in Roman Leicester

The Anubis Box (top left)
This small, rectangular ivory panel found in the courtyard house on Vine Street is from a box. It is an extraordinary find. Relief-carved ivory boxes are extremely rare discoveries and this fragment is exceptional because of its design. Unusually, instead of belonging to a classical tradition, it depicts the Egyptian god Anubis squatting amongst lotus flowers and grasping a lance in his right hand.

Roman Egypt had a long-established industry producing ivory boxes, but most were decorated with Greek and Roman, rather than Egyptian, gods. Anubis was popular amongst Egyptian soldiers in the Roman army and the fact that the figure on this panel is holding a lance may hint at a military connection. This box would have been an exceedingly rare luxury item even in Egypt, so for it to have made its way to Roman Britain is remarkable.

It is not the only link between the courtyard house and the eastern parts of the Roman Empire. Another discovery was a lead seal belonging to the *III Cyrenaica*, a legion which only served in Egypt and what is now Syria. This is further evidence that goods and people travelled all the way across the Empire, and it suggests that one of the building's inhabitants might have included a wealthy military officer who had served in the eastern legions before moving to Roman Britain.

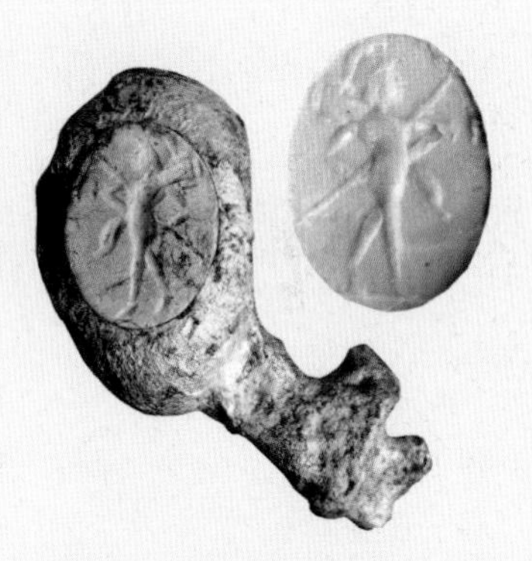

The Mars Intaglio (right)
Another object found on Vine Street was a once-splendid silver ring containing a semi-precious gemstone upon which an image, or intaglio, had been carved. At some point the ring was almost destroyed in an intense fire which distorted and melted the silver and discoloured the stone, but the well-carved image survived. The figure is that of the Roman god Mars, depicted naked apart from a helmet and cloak, and carrying a spear and trophy. This is the persona *Mars Gravidus,* which the god was believed to take on when guiding armies to victory. Rings like this were fashionable in the 1st and 2nd centuries AD and the stone, although discoloured by the heat, was probably red jasper.

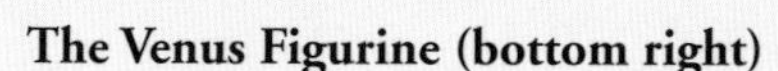

The Venus Figurine (bottom right)
This broken torso from a small white-clay votive figurine was found behind the courtyard house on Vine Street. It depicts the Roman goddess Venus and when intact would have showed her holding a tress of hair with her right hand whilst her left hand clutched a cloth draped over or beside her leg. These were cheap figurines made in central Gaul and were often presented as offerings to the gods at temples or kept in household shrines. They were particularly associated with women during childbirth.

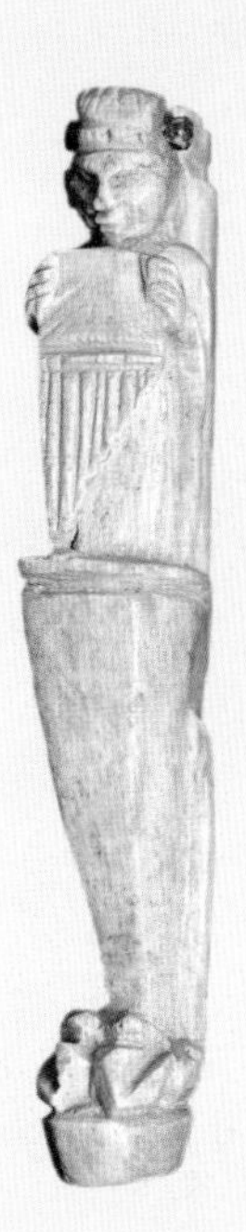

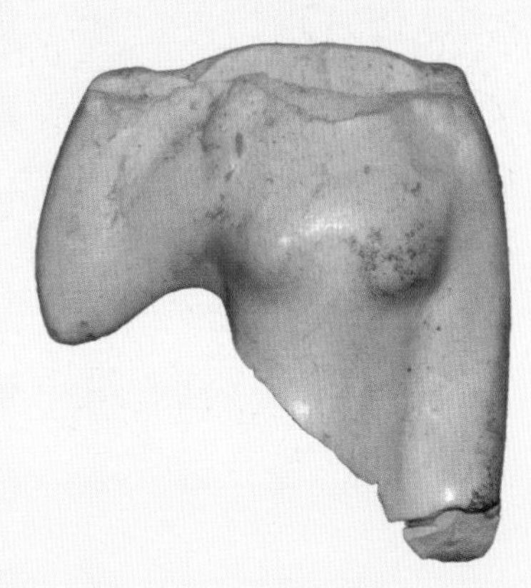

The Pan Clasp Knife (bottom left)
During earlier excavations beneath the original Shires shopping centre, this complete, carved bone handle for a folding knife was found. Such handles are relatively scarce in Roman Britain. The upper part shows a small, grotesque figure holding a set of pan-pipes as if he is about to play. The figure is probably Pan, god of shepherds and flocks, mountains, hunting and rustic music, or one of the other part-animal followers of the god Dionysus. The knife may have belonged to a farmer or someone who worshipped the gods of the countryside.

The End of Roman Leicester and the Arrival of the Anglo-Saxons
(early 5th to mid 7th century AD)

The early years of the 5th century AD saw considerable political upheaval within the western Roman Empire. By 410, the remaining Roman troops and government officials had withdrawn from Britain and the province was left to defend itself from increasing numbers of raids by barbarian tribes, particularly the Angles, Saxons and Jutes from what is now northern Germany and Denmark. We can only guess at what effect this had on life in Roman Leicester. Although the inhabitants perhaps tried to carry on as normal, the monetary economy must have collapsed relatively quickly as trade with the Roman Empire ceased and coin supplies from the continent dried up. Without civic authority, public buildings and streets must soon have fallen into decay.

At present, it is not possible to recognise and date any activity at all between 400 and 450 on archaeological sites in Leicester, but this is probably because the inhabitants of the city were still using the same pottery and other objects as they had before. It used to be thought that thick layers of dark soil found above the latest Roman levels showed that the town was abandoned, but scientific analysis now suggests that this accumulated as a result of domestic occupation and the keeping of animals. The discovery within the walls of Roman Leicester of distinctive hand-made pottery and other finds, such as brooches (**right**), of 5th–6th century date would seem to indicate the arrival of Anglo-Saxon settlers. Quite what effect this had on the pre-existing population is not entirely certain, but perhaps they gradually became integrated with the newcomers and began to adopt their objects and way of life.

The general vicinity of modern Highcross Leicester seems to have been targeted for occupation in the early Anglo-Saxon period, perhaps because it was an area of open ground in the still-walled Roman town which had not been fully developed. The recent excavations have revealed the remains of four buildings of this period on Highcross Street and Vaughan Way, all constructed of timber, with floors suspended over large pits, probably used for storage or insulation. Archaeologists generally refer to these as 'sunken-featured buildings'. Whilst some of them may have been lived in, we know from other sites that they were often used as workshops, particularly for the manufacture of textiles. This is based on the discovery of objects associated with weaving, such as loom weights, spindle whorls and combs – like the one from nearby St Peter's Lane (see page 41) – which may have come from a disturbed building. The early Anglo-Saxon building on Highcross Street (**3**) was constructed in the rubble (**2**) of the east wall of the *macellum* (**1**) which had collapsed in the 5th century (see page 23).

On rural Anglo-Saxon sites, sunken-featured buildings are often associated with larger rectangular halls constructed with posts set into the ground. A large structure of this type on Vine Street could be an Anglo-Saxon hall built next to the ruins of the Roman courtyard house, and there are also traces of what may be a similar structure on Sanvey Gate.

Left: An Anglo-Saxon building found on Highcross Street. It was built on fallen masonry next to the ruined Roman macellum in the 5th–6th century AD.

Above: Two early Anglo-Saxon brooches of a type which broadly dates to the 5th and 6th century AD. Reproduced at actual size.

Early Anglo-Saxon Settlement Outside the Town Walls
(5th to 7th century AD)

As well as Anglo-Saxon occupation within the Roman walls of *Ratae*, there is also evidence of 5th to 7th century settlement outside the south gate (**1**) alongside the Roman road which led from Leicester to Caves Inn on the Warwickshire border (the Roman town of *Tripontium*). Large timber buildings (**2**) have been found beneath De Montfort University's campus along with pottery and other finds suggesting that the spinning of yarn and the weaving of cloth were taking place (**3**). This would have been an everyday task in the Anglo-Saxon period when yarn was needed to produce cloth on the looms which were set up in nearly every house (**4**).

Middle to Late Anglo-Saxon and Danish Leicester
(early 7th to mid 11th century AD)

Although it is unlikely that the first Anglo-Saxons to have lived in Leicester occupied anything like what we (or the Roman inhabitants) would recognise as a town, the community must have flourished as the bishopric of the Middle Angles was established here in the 670s. It is thought that the cathedral may have been beneath the present St Nicholas Church, on the site of the Roman baths, the Jewry Wall forming its western end. This high-status building may have been a focus for markets and fairs, but so far we have no clear archaeological evidence for settlement in Leicester between the late 7th and mid 9th centuries.

Viking raids began in the early 9th century and by 877, England was divided between the Saxon-held south and a large part of northern and eastern England known as the Danelaw, which was under the control of Danish Vikings. Leicester became one of the five Boroughs of the Danelaw until it was recaptured by Lady Aetheflaed in 918. The Danish interlude seems to have left little trace, apart from a few Scandinavian-style artefacts and many street names ending in 'gate' from the Danish *gata* or 'street'. Finds of late 9th–11th century pottery and fragments of timber buildings show that settlement had begun to develop along a route between the Roman north and south gates (what is now Highcross Street) and soon spread eastwards into the area of Highcross Leicester. It is thought that the church of St Peter and probably several others were founded before the Norman Conquest, suggesting a growing population.

Far left: Looking towards the old Roman town from the south through the Anglo-Saxon suburb as it may have been during the 6th century AD. The inset illustrates the types of activities taking place inside the buildings.

Above: An Anglo-Saxon bone comb found on St Peter's Lane beneath the old Shires shopping centre. Reproduced at actual size.

Left: A silver penny minted in York during the reign of Eadgar the Peaceful who ruled England between AD 959 and 975. It was found near St Peter's Church. Reproduced at twice actual size.

Medieval Leicester
(mid-11th to mid-16th century AD)

By the time of the Norman Conquest in 1066, Leicester was once again a thriving town and the Domesday Book of 1086 records that there were 322 houses and six churches, suggesting that the population was perhaps between 1500 and 2000. The castle was almost certainly built by William the Conqueror in 1068 whilst on his expedition to crush northern resistance. It was located in a dominant position, next to the river and at the corner of the Roman town walls. In the 12th–13th centuries, Leicester seems to have undergone a development boom. Several major new buildings appeared both inside and outside the walls, such as the friaries and Leicester Abbey, whilst many existing buildings, including the castle and the churches, were enlarged or rebuilt. Although we know that there must also have been a massive expansion in the number of households in the borough – shown on excavations by numerous cess pits, wells and rubbish pits in the back yards of properties – evidence for the houses themselves is extremely rare because they were built of perishable materials (like timber, mud and thatch) which have not survived. There were also a few stone buildings like one found on the site of the BBC building in St Nicholas Place. This may have been the home of a wealthy merchant in the 12th century and occupied a large plot on the principal trading street of the town, the medieval High Street (now Highcross Street). It had an undercroft built of stone and re-used Roman tile with narrow windows, which was probably used for the storage of valuable goods. In 1265, Leicester passed to a line of wealthy Lancastrian earls who undertook further ambitious building projects such as that of the Newarke, a religious precinct south of the castle.

The picture (**left**) shows a bird's eye view of medieval Leicester from the north-east as it may have appeared in about 1450. In many senses (sight, sound and smell) the urban space must have been almost rural in character, with quite a few landmark trees (known from documents), livestock and of course a lot of mud. By this time, many of the streets which still exist today had been established, together with most of the main plots, which were generally long and narrow, extending back from the street frontage by as much as 40m. Until about the 13th century, the layout of streets and property boundaries was influenced to a considerable extent by the surviving remains of Roman structures. The medieval High Street, for example, respects the corner of the Roman *forum* suggesting that the walls were still visible, whilst some boundaries and medieval buildings seem to have re-used Roman walls as part of their construction. We know from the accounts of later writers that even in the 16th century, almost all of the buildings in Leicester – with the exception of churches and some public buildings – were timber-framed, with panels infilled with wattle and daub and with roofs of slate, shingle or thatch. Many such buildings survived into the 19th and 20th centuries and some were recorded in photographs and drawings, providing an invaluable record of the medieval town.

The Roman town walls were maintained throughout the medieval period and the external ditches were also re-dug regularly, but by the later 15th century the defences gradually began to be pulled down and the stone carted away. Suburbs had developed outside each of the four gates into the town, whilst the north-eastern part of the area inside the walls – the back lanes – seems to have declined from the early 14th century leaving large open spaces given over to orchards and horticulture. Surrounding the town were the three great open fields (west, south and east) which provided produce for the inhabitants and grazing for livestock.

Left: Looking towards medieval Leicester from the north-east as it may have been during the mid 15th century

Right: The faces of Leicester? Some of the carved wooden heads which decorate the 15th-century roof of the north aisle in All Saints' Church which is situated on Highcross Street.

The Castle, the Newarke and the South Suburb

A castle was built in about 1068 inside the south-west corner of the town, and became the centre of power for the first Norman overlord of Leicester, Hugh de Grentmaisnil, allowing him to maintain a hold on the town and the surrounding area. The castle consisted of a large mound of earth or motte (**1**) topped with a timber tower, and an area enclosed by a ditch and bank known as a bailey, which probably contained a hall, chapel and ancillary buildings. In 1107 Robert de Beaumont, first Earl of Leicester, established a college of canons (community of priests) at St Mary de Castro (**2**) and probably rebuilt the castle defences in stone. The second earl, Robert le Bossu, built the Great Hall in about 1150 (**3**). This was an immense stone aisled building with a timber roof supported on oak posts (**below**) and still survives today, although much altered. At its northern end was a raised timber platform or dais where the lord and high-ranking retainers would have sat. A door behind the dais led to the lord's private apartments whilst at the south end there was access to a separate kitchen above an undercroft (John of Gaunt's Cellar), where ale, wine and food would have been stored. Following a revolt in 1173, in which the third earl, Robert Blanchmains, was a leading conspirator, Leicester was besieged and captured by Henry II who later ordered the destruction of the castle and town defences. Although excavations have suggested that this was put into effect in a limited way, the Great Hall and other buildings seem to have been spared.

The castle later became the residence of the earls, later dukes, of Lancaster and reached its greatest extent in the 14th century. The accounts refer to many other buildings which have long since disappeared, and there was also a herb garden (**4**) and a watermill (**5**) in what is now Castle Gardens. In 1399, Leicester Castle ceased to be a ducal residence when the second Duke of Lancaster became King Henry IV, and it began to fall into decline.

South of the castle lay the Newarke or 'New Work' (**6**), founded by Henry Earl of Lancaster in 1330–1, starting with the establishment of Trinity Hospital (**7**) to care for the elderly and infirm. Later in the 14th century, the Newarke became the home of a college of priests and contained chantry houses, priest's houses, a vicarage and the church of the Annunciation of the Blessed Virgin Mary (**8**), completed by 1361. A 16th-century visitor said 'the College Church is not very great, but it is exceeding fair'. It contained several chapels, marble tombs of notable Lancastrians and other benefactors and had a cloister on its south-west side. A few arches of the church survive today in the basement of the Hawthorn Building of De Montfort University. In around 1400, the Newarke was enclosed by a substantial stone wall, with a monumental entrance (**9**) – now known as The Magazine Gateway. A smaller gate, the Turret Gateway (**10**), separated the Newarke from the Castle. About a hundred years after this picture, the Newarke College was dissolved by Henry VIII and the church, as well as many other buildings, was demolished.

Next to the Newarke was the south suburb. Although there had been a settlement here in the early Anglo-Saxon period, this did not last and it was not until the 12th century that a suburb began to develop outside the medieval south gate (**11**). Documents tell us that it was a poor area and archaeological excavations have shown that by the 15th century, it was a focus for some of the more unpleasant and polluting industries, such as the processing of animal hides and skins.

Left: The castle, the Newarke and the south suburb as they may have been during the mid 15th century.

Right: Goddard's painting of the interior of the Great Hall in 1821.

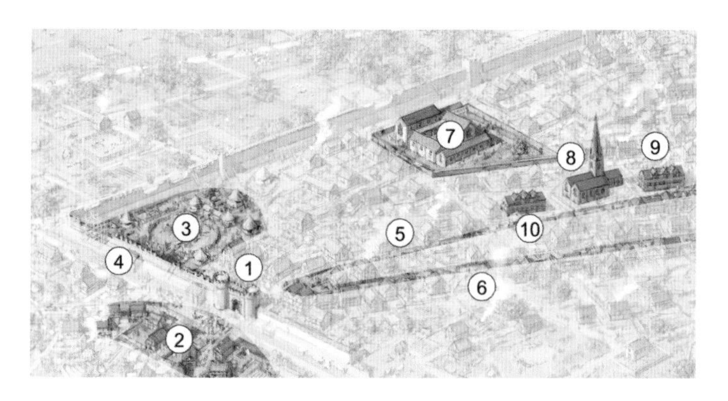

The South-East Quarter

The ancient Roman gates of Leicester, probably built in the 3rd century AD, are very likely to have survived into the medieval period, albeit much repaired and altered (**1**). By the 15th century, their prime function was probably for the collection of tolls from traders coming into the town rather than defence. From time to time, the large iron-strapped wooden gates would be closed to prevent the escape of fugitives or animals from the town. The gates were also symbols of the wealth and status of the borough and above each archway, the royal arms were displayed. Chambers above the gates were a source of revenue for the borough as they were rented out during the medieval period. The narrowness and lack of height of the gates may have been a factor in the development of the Haymarket outside the East Gate, which contributed to the prosperity of the medieval east suburb (**2**). This was because loaded wagons of hay could not pass through the arch. The gates were all demolished in 1774.

In this part of Leicester, most of today's streets follow the same lines as their medieval predecessors. Much of this corner of the medieval walled town was taken up by the Saturday Market (**3**), established as early as 1298 and occupying an area much larger than the current market-place. As now, the market offered a wide range of products for sale – not only foodstuffs such as grain, beans, meat and fish but also wool, clothing and drapery in the 'Housewives' Market'. On the east side of the market-place was the corn wall (**4**), where farmers would display samples of their grain, whilst to the north was the Sheepmarket (**5**), modern Silver Street, and the Swinesmarket (**6**), modern High Street.

The Greyfriars (Franciscan Friars) were established in Leicester in the 12th century and occupied a large walled precinct west of the market-place (**7**), with gateways onto what is now Peacock Lane and Friar Lane. Its main claim to fame is that its church was the burial place of Richard III following the Battle of Bosworth. The friary was dissolved in the reign of Henry VIII and demolished not long afterwards. Very little is known about the arrangement of buildings on the site and all that survives today is a fragment of the precinct wall.

In the 13th century, St Martin's Church (**8**) – now the Cathedral – was Leicester's wealthiest parish church. It is shown here flanked by two large buildings. On the right is the Guildhall (**9**), built as the meeting place of the Guild of Corpus Christi in about 1390, and to the left was the hall of the Guild of St George (**10**). Guilds were associations of craftsmen and merchants; they were part trade unions, part secret societies and part charities. Corpus Christi was the leading guild in Leicester and in the later 15th century its two masters had considerable influence over the mayor and council of the borough. By 1494–5, the Borough Corporation began using the hall for their meetings. The Guildhall continued to be Leicester's Town Hall until it was replaced in the 19th century with the present building in Horsefair Street. The Guild of St George was much poorer and less influential. It was probably chiefly responsible for organising processions featuring St George and the Dragon.

Left: The south-eastern quarter as it may have been during the mid 15th century.

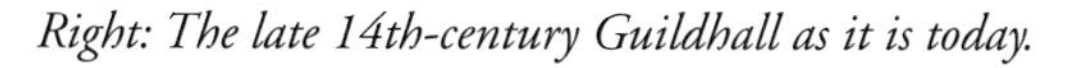

Right: The late 14th-century Guildhall as it is today.

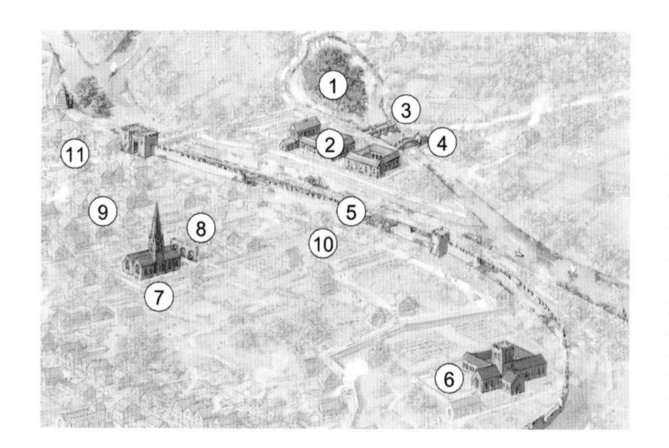

The West Side of Town

In the past, the River Soar flowed in a series of channels, creating small islands just beyond the town walls (**1**). On one of these, the Augustinians established their friary in 1254 (**2**). Documents record that they had built their church by 1306 and excavations in 1973–78 showed that there were two cloisters to the north of it, separated by a wide drain. The southern cloister was the larger of the two and on its northern and eastern sides were the refectory and dormitory ranges respectively. The smaller cloister had buildings on its western, northern and eastern sides. Two bridges crossed the western arm of the Soar near the friary. Bow Bridge carried the road to Hinckley (**3**) whilst the smaller Little Bow Bridge (**4**) gave the friars access to a close containing St Augustine's Well. The friary was dissolved in 1538 and all of its buildings had been demolished by 1542–3.

Excavations have revealed the line of the western town defences and shown that even in the medieval period, most of the fabric of the wall was of Roman construction, built of strongly mortared granite and about 2.5m thick. As with the castle, the archaeological evidence suggests only partial destruction of the town defences after the rebellion of 1173, and sections of the wall seem to have been pulled down or 'slighted', but were later rebuilt (**5**). Within the walls, much of the land in this part of town was occupied by the Dominican friars, the Blackfriars, who came to Leicester in the mid 13th century, taking over an existing church, St Clement's (**6**), said to have been very poor by this time. The friary was dissolved by Henry VIII and the church was demolished soon after 1536. So far, only a fragment of the precinct wall has been revealed by excavation.

St Nicholas' Church (**7**) contains the remains of two windows which date from the 10th century, but there are good reasons for thinking that it was founded much earlier than this. It is believed originally to have been dedicated to St Augustine (the first Christian missionary to Britain in the 6th century) and excavation has shown that it was once attached to the adjacent Roman Jewry Wall (**8**). An attractive theory is that St Nicholas' Church is the site of Leicester's middle Saxon cathedral, built in the 7th–8th century amidst the ruins of the Roman bath complex, with the Jewry Wall forming part of its structure and the Roman plunge pools perhaps even being used for Christian baptism. This would help explain why the Jewry Wall, unlike all other major Roman structures in Leicester, has survived to the present day.

The sale of meat in the medieval period was concentrated in the butchers' 'shambles' close to St Nicholas' Church (**9**). The nearby street 'Holy Bones' may have been so-named because of discarded butchers' waste. It is probably no coincidence that nearby land, close to the river, between Blackfriars and the West Bridge, has been shown by excavation to have contained one or more tanneries (**10**). The skins of sheep were normally de-haired by the fellmongers before being sold on to the tawyer to be processed into leather, whilst tanners exclusively processed the hides of cattle.

A focal point of the town was the Wednesday Market, located at the junction of what is now Highcross Street and High Street. It was marked in the 16th century by the stone Highcross, one column of which survives today in the present market-place. Leading up to this crossroads from the West Gate was 'Hot Gate' (**11**) – so called because the earl of Leicester's ovens were located in the vicinity.

Left: The west side of the town as it may have been during the mid 15th century.

Right: A late 13th- or 14th-century leather shoe found in Leicester. It had been thrown away because its sole had worn through. The shoe is 21½cm long which is equivalent to an adult size '1' today.

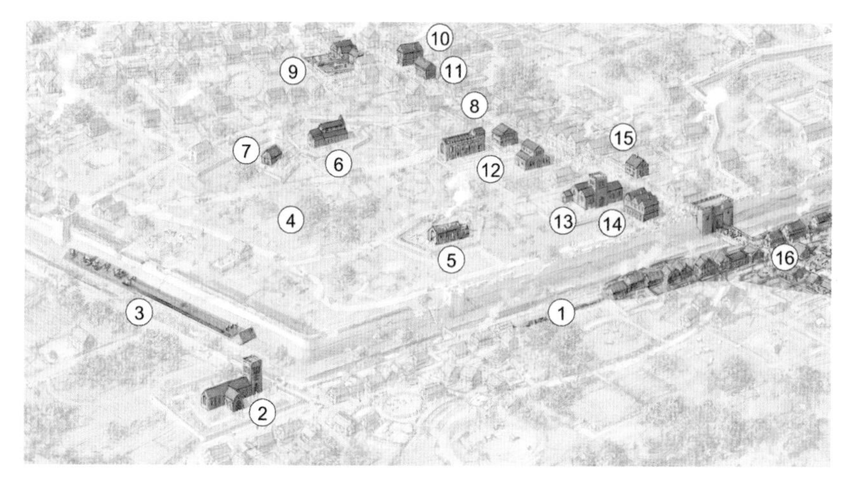

The North-East Quarter and the North Suburb

Running along the north side of the town is Sanvey Gate (**1**), known as 'le Skeyth' in medieval times, and possibly a route for religious processions from Northgates to St Margaret's Church (**2**). This parish church was unusual in that it was in a suburb which owed feudal allegiance to the Bishop of Lincoln rather than the Earl of Leicester. Close to St Margaret's, alongside the town wall (by now patched with mud and straw), were the butts for practising archery (**3**) – a legal requirement for all men between the age of 15 and 60 in the medieval period. At the time of this picture, the land was leased from the Crown at the annual rent of one barbed arrow.

Although many people had lived in the north-east quarter in the 12th and 13th centuries, in the 14th century the population seems to have started to decline (**4**). This may have resulted from starvation caused by a series of disastrous harvests between 1300 and 1310 and later, from the large numbers of deaths from plague – the Black Death – which struck Leicester in 1348. The area then seems to have been turned over to orchards and gardens and few people lived in this part of town again until the late 18th century. This is reflected by the fate of two of the town's churches – St Michael's, demolished by the middle of the 15th century (**5**) and St Peter's (**6**), which held out a little longer being kept in repair in the early years of the 16th century. It was finally pulled down in 1573 and the materials used to build a new school (see page 63). Next to it was a building constructed of timber and mud that may have been the vicarage (7).

The medieval High Street (now Highcross Street, **8**) continued to be the main focus of occupation in the northern part of Leicester – it was a busy thoroughfare and the town's main trading street. Towards the top of the picture, on the eastern side of the street, the Highcross Street excavation (**9**) revealed a plot which had been used for brewing ale on a commercial scale at this time. It no doubt had much custom from the nearby Wednesday Market and may have supplied alehouses such as the large and elaborate 15th-century timber-framed building opposite, later known as the Blue Boar Inn (**10**), where Richard III is reputed to have stayed the night before the battle of Bosworth in 1485. To the north was another inn, later known as the Admiral Rodney (**11**). Further north along Highcross Street, a group of buildings represent the hospital of the College of St John the Evangelist and St John the Baptist (**12**). This had been founded by at least the 12th century and had its own church, part of which survived into the 18th century

Next to All Saints Church (**13**) is a medieval timber-framed building with three gables (**14**). Parts of this building, later known as the Cross Keys Inn, survive today and have been tree-ring dated to the 14th century. On the other side of Highcross Street, a stone building known from recent excavations may be the vicarage of All Saints' (**15**). The road led out of the North Gate to the north suburb (**16**), where the dyers and fullers occupied land next to the river, and after crossing two bridges it reached the church of St Leonard before forking eastwards to the Abbey and west to Charnwood Forest.

Left: The north-east quarter and the north suburb as they may have been during the mid 15th century.

Right: A 19th-century lithograph of the Blue Boar Inn on Highcross Street by the artist John Flower. The Admiral Rodney Inn can also be seen in the background.

The Parish of St Michael and its Church

According to documentary records, the parish church of St Michael once stood in the medieval town's north-east quarter. It has long been considered one of Leicester's 'lost' parish churches, the others being St Clement's and St Peter's (see pages 49 and 55) all of which ceased to exist at some time before 1600.

Until the recent excavations on Vine Street, it was supposed that St Michael's church had been founded before the Norman Conquest of 1066. This theory has now been disproved, as excavation has shown that the churchyard and surrounding area were waste ground during the 11th and much of the 12th century, occupied only by the ruins of Roman buildings (**1**). By the middle of the 12th century, most of these ruins had been cleared and their footings systematically quarried for stone. This was probably used in the construction of Leicester Abbey, founded in 1143 (or possibly as early as 1139), to the north of the town, which owned the land. Burials only began to occur at St Michael's towards the end of the 12th century and this ties in with the first known reference to the church which dates to 1200.

In the 12th century, occupation seems to have expanded away from the main streets into previously empty areas. In the north-east quarter of the town, gravelled streets began to appear and stone and timber houses were built (**2**). One of the streets, St Michael's Lane, still survives today as part of Burgess Street (**3**). At the same time wells were being dug, outhouses erected and small fenced enclosures, probably animal pens, created. Yet uncharacteristically for an urban setting, this new development was one of detached buildings, each set in its own smallholding, rather than the densely packed rows of buildings which fronted narrow burgage plots along the town's main streets (see page 61).

With an expanding population, it is easy to see why a new church was established in this part of town. Evidence for the church itself proved frustratingly elusive and the only clues to the building were a few degraded fragments of mud and stone walls west of St Michael's Lane. These suggest that the church was a small timber building (**4**), which fits well with an account of 1220 that the church was 'very poor'. By the mid 13th century a small stone porch had been added to the west end of the church and it also had a small bell turret, as we know from documents that in 1490 the bell was re-hung in All Saints' Church.

St Michael's Church was surrounded by a graveyard which stretched south around the remains of a large Roman building (**5**). This building appears to have been deliberately left standing through the period the cemetery was in use, as no burials were found inside it. This suggests that it may have been partially occupied in the medieval period, and it may even have been used as the vicarage for St Michael's, which was established in 1222.

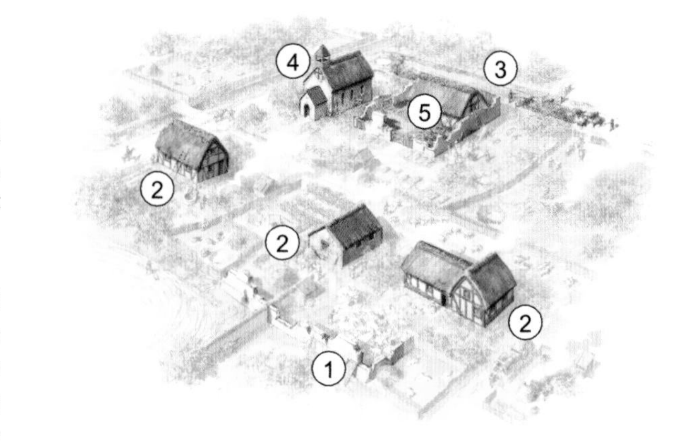

Left: Looking across Vine Street from the south as it may have been during the mid 13th century AD.

Above: A late medieval brooch or badge in the shape of a bird, lost near St Michael's church in the 14th century. Reproduced at twice actual size.

St Peter's Church

The site of St Peter's Church (**1**) and its graveyard (**2**) was discovered off Vaughan Way, where the John Lewis store now stands. It was the second 'lost' medieval church in Leicester found during recent excavations. It had been assumed that it was small and poorly provided for, like its neighbour St Michael's, given its location within the back lanes. However, excavation showed that this was not in fact the case and although little remained of the building, St Peter's was clearly much more substantial than St Michael's. Built of stone, the church was gradually enlarged over the centuries, representing a considerable investment on the part of its parishioners.

Most of the plan of the church was uncovered, enabling the archaeologists to establish how it had developed over time. The church probably first took the form of a simple, two-celled building consisting of a small nave (the area where the congregation worshipped) and chancel (the area where the priests conducted the service) sometime in the late 10th or 11th century. Radiocarbon dating of burials shows that the graveyard, at least, had been in use since the 10th century. In the 12th century, the nave was enlarged with a substantial extension (**a**) and by the end of the century a bell turret had also been added to its west end (**3** and **b**). A pit in which a large bell had been cast was found under the turret. Burnt stones in the pit were subjected to archaeomagnetic dating, which showed that the bell had been made at some point between 1150 and 1180. During the following century, aisles were added to the north and south side of the nave (**c**) and by the 14th century the parish was prosperous enough to afford building a much large chancel (**d**) at the east end. By the time the church reached its peak in the 15th century (**e**), the south aisle had been widened and additional rooms had been added to the north (**4**) and to the south of the chancel. One of these was a small charnel house, or ossuary, which housed stacked bones from at least eighty-two people (see page 11). These bones had been collected and stored when grave diggers disturbed earlier burials. The church was finally demolished in 1573.

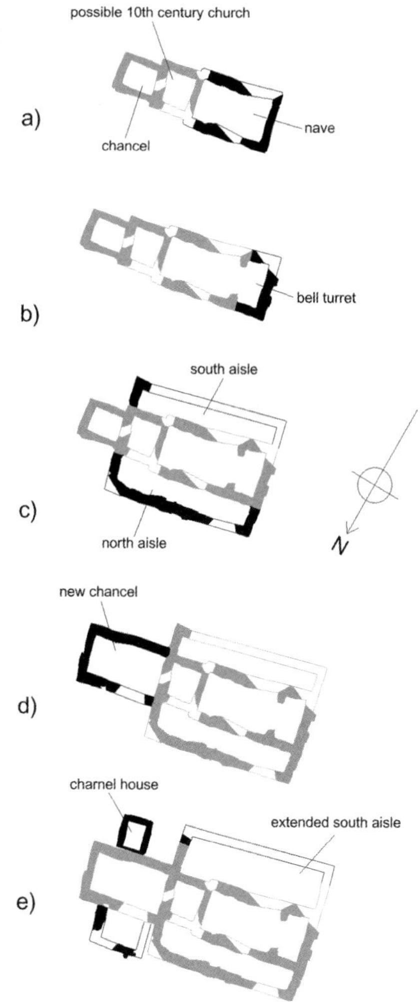

The excavation also revealed a sequence of buildings east of the church (**5**). The earliest in timber, with a cellar, was constructed in the 11th century. A large stone hall was added in the 12th century, but by the early 14th century, both buildings had been demolished, probably to make way for the newly enlarged chancel. They were replaced by a series of timber and mud-walled buildings which remained until the late 16th century, after which they were abandoned and left to collapse. It is thought that these structures may have been the church's vicarage, first mentioned in documents in 1226.

Left: View of St Peter's Church from the north-west as it may have looked during the 15th century.

Right: A late 14th-century floor tile from the church. It is decorated with the coat-of-arms of the House of Lancaster which had close ties with the town, the Duke of Lancaster also being the Earl of Leicester.

Far right: The five main building phases St Peter's Church underwent between the 12th century and the 16th century.

Leicester's Medieval Graveyards

Two large medieval cemeteries were uncovered on the site of the Highcross Leicester development – the graveyards for the churches of St Peter's and St Michael's. In total 1,590 skeletons were carefully exhumed (**left**), making this one of the largest investigations of medieval graveyards in the East Midlands, and providing a rare opportunity to examine the health and lifestyle of many of the inhabitants of medieval Leicester.

Burial rites could be diverse during the medieval period. In St Peter's graveyard, the burials were generally orientated west–east (with the head to the west) and most individuals were probably simply wrapped in a shroud of cloth (which did not survive) before being placed in the grave. The remains of iron nails in some of the graves shows that timber coffins were sometimes used, whilst other burials seem to have been in stone-lined graves or placed on a layer of charcoal or ash. The variety of burial practices in St Peter's graveyard is partly a reflection of how long the cemetery was in use, burial traditions changing over the centuries, but it also shows that some of the church's parishioners could afford more elaborate funerals. This contrasts with St Michael's graveyard, where only simple shroud burials were found, suggesting it was a poorer parish than St Peter's. As was the custom with medieval Christian burials, the majority of individuals in both graveyards were interred without grave goods. There were, however, two notable exceptions, both found inside St Peter's Church. One was a skeleton with a coin of Edward I (1272–1307) placed inside its mouth, harking back to pre-Christian practices, and another was buried with a lead papal seal, or *bulla*, of Pope Innocent VI (1352–62), see page 58. Both of these individuals were probably important members of the local community.

Other burials bear witness to poignant moments and tragedies. One woman had received a severe blow to the front of her head, which had probably killed her, and in one corner of St Peter's graveyard, a mass grave containing over twenty people was uncovered (**bottom right**). Most of those buried in this grave were under 13 years of age and all bore signs of poor health and malnutrition, making it likely that they had all died during an epidemic.

Approximately 40% of the burials were male and 60% were female. The average height of the men was 5ft 7in (1.71m) whilst that of women was 5ft 2in (1.59m). The majority had died between the age of thirty-two and fifty, but on the whole women tended to live a little longer than men, with more living past the age of fifty. However, more women than men died during young adulthood, possibly due to the dangers of childbearing. Child mortality was especially high, with approximately a quarter of those who died being under the age of 12. Most of the individuals had led a hard life involving a lot of lifting, bending and carrying, and nearly half of the adults showed signs of osteoarthritis. Dental health was poor and many people had dental hypoplasia, an indication of poor health during childhood. Evidence of rickets and anaemia were also both present and nearly 10% of the population were affected by infectious diseases, including tuberculosis and syphilis.

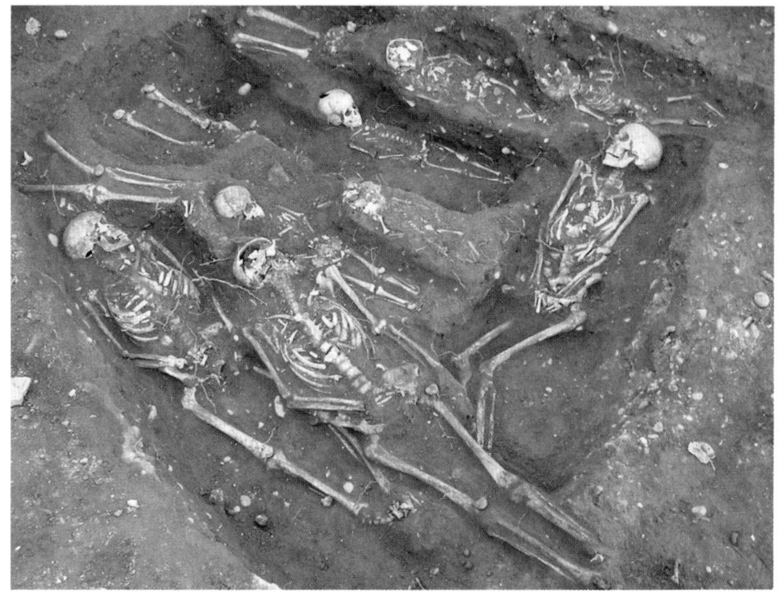

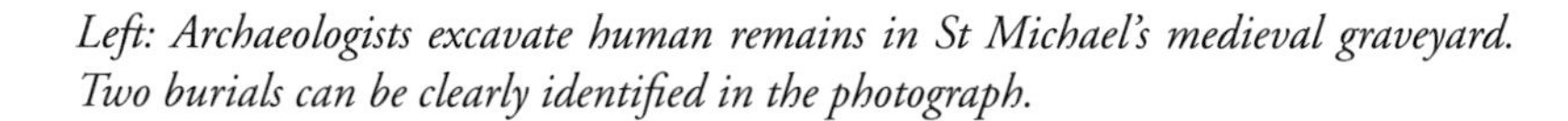

Left: Archaeologists excavate human remains in St Michael's medieval graveyard. Two burials can be clearly identified in the photograph.

Right: A mass-grave found in one corner of St Peter's graveyard. It contained people who had all died during an epidemic. This was not the plague. Carbon dating indicated that this epidemic occurred during the latter half of the 12th century, nearly two hundred years before the Black Death reached England.

Two Christian Symbols From Medieval Leicester

The Papal Bulla of Pope Innocent VI (left)

This papal *bulla,* found in St Peter's Church, would originally have been attached by a cord to the bottom of a letter or charter issued by Pope Innocent VI between 1352 and 1362 to authenticate it. In this case, the *bulla* was probably attached to a Papal Indulgence – a document issued by the Catholic Church as a sign that a temporal punishment for a sin had been fully or partially reduced. Indulgences were only issued after a sinner had confessed and received absolution. They were very popular during the medieval period as a reward for specific acts of good work or prayer. This one was found beside the skeleton of a middle-aged woman who had been buried beneath the nave of the church.

The circular lead disc depicts the founders of the Church of Rome, the apostles Peter and Paul. They can be identified by the letters SPASPE (*Sanctus Paulus and Sanctus Petrus*) above the two bearded faces. On the reverse (bottom left) is the name of the pope, in this instance INNO CETIVS PP VI or Pope Innocent VI, PP being the abbreviated Latin for *Papa* (father) meaning Pope.

The practice of being buried with a papal indulgence was fashionable in Britain during the 14th century. This was the time when the worst ravages of the plague were sweeping across England. People were becoming increasingly anxious about the possibility of a sudden death and concerned about their spiritual wellbeing. The rite appears to have been especially favoured by women and the location of their graves often suggests they were important members of their communities.

The Crucifix (below)

This small copper arm, just 50mm long, was found during the excavation of St Peter's graveyard. It is the left arm from an effigy of Christ nailed to a wooden cross; it is estimated that the figure would originally have been about 11cm tall.

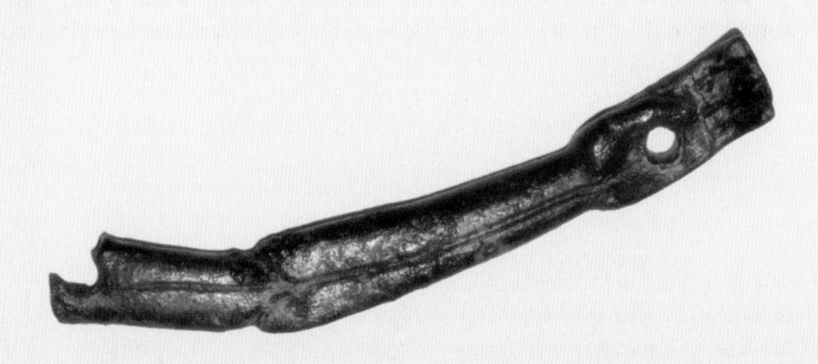

Leisure in Medieval Leicester

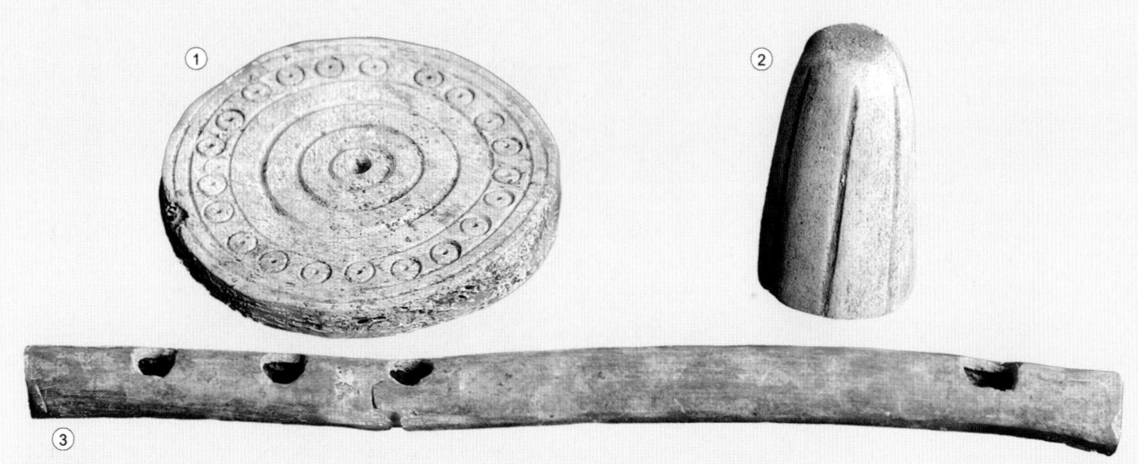

The excavations have provided only tantalising glimpses of leisure activities in medieval Leicester, but the few artefacts which have been found show a range of pastimes.

Amongst the finds were counters from two 12th-century board games. One was a carved bone disc which could have been used as a counter in 'Tables' (**1**), a popular game similar to backgammon. The other game piece was carved from antler and appeared to be a pawn from an early chess set (**2**).

Parts of two musical instruments were also identified. One was an ivory tuning peg from an open-framed instrument such as a harp or a fiddle, whilst the other was a simple bone flute (**3**). The flute was made from bone, probably from the wing of a goose, and was found in a late 13th-century pit near St Michael's Church. Tuning pegs were evidently easily lost as 11 more were found during the excavation of the original Shires shopping centre.

Several arrowheads of the type used with longbows were also found near St Peter's Church and along Highcross Street. These may be evidence of hunting, but may also bear witness to the need for constant practice in order to be skilled in the use of a longbow. One arrowhead was discovered in a grave in St Peter's churchyard and it may have been deliberately placed on the body at burial.

Winter activities are illustrated by the discovery of a late 13th century bone ice-skate near St Michael's church (**below**). This was carved from the leg bone of a horse or cow and would have been tied to the bottom of a shoe by leather thongs threaded through holes drilled at either end. Medieval skating was not like modern skating. Bone skates did not have sharp gliding edges like modern skates so momentum on the ice was often achieved using metal-tipped poles, more akin to cross-country skiing. This was wonderfully described in the late 12th century by William Fitz Stephen, a secretary to the Archbishop of Canterbury Thomas à Becket (**right**).

The Art of Medieval Ice-skating

'...when the great marsh...is frozen over, numerous bands of young men go out to play on the ice. They arrange their feet at a set distance, and gaining additional rapidity as they move, they traverse enormous space... Others of them are more knowing in their play, for they fit the leg-bones of animals to their feet, binding them firmly around their ankles, and hold in their hands poles shod with iron, which they strike against the ice, and thus impel themselves on it with the swiftness of a bird or a ball from an engine [cannon]. Sometimes it is agreed that two of them shall advance one against the other in this way from a great distance; they rush together, each lifts his staff to strike the other, and the contest ends by one or both falling, and receiving some severe bodily injury...'

From William Fitz Stephen's description of the city of London in 1173 in his *Life of Saint Thomas of Canterbury*

A Medieval Brewery on Highcross Street

Modern Highcross Street was the principal street of medieval Leicester, confusingly known then as 'High Street' whilst the present-day High Street was known as 'Swinesmarket'. The Highcross Street site provided a rare opportunity to investigate a medieval street frontage – usually frontages either lie buried under the pavement following road widening, or have been destroyed by later cellars. The excavations revealed a whole sequence of medieval and post-medieval buildings set out in long narrow properties known as 'burgage plots', which extended back from the street.

The earliest structures were slight timber buildings dating to the later 9th or 10th century, the first of this period to be found in Leicester. By the 12th century they had been replaced with more substantial timber-framed buildings resting on stone footings (**1**), and by the late 13th century long stone boundary walls had been built to separate the plots (**2**), which were continuously occupied until the 21st century.

In the yards behind the buildings were refuse pits, stone privies (**3**) and other structures. During the 14th century the yard behind one building contained a series of stone ovens and kilns associated with brewing. These were walled off from the rest of the plot leaving a narrow passage (**4**) which would have led to an alleyway at the rear – allowing goods to be moved in and out without going through the building on the street. Brewing, for instance, used large amounts of water which would have needed to be brought in from elsewhere before the days of piped supplies. Weak ale (by modern standards) was widely consumed during the medieval period as it was much safer to drink than water from wells which were often contaminated. Many small, back-yard breweries would have been scattered across the town, and tax records for the year 1339 alone list a total of 170 brewers in Leicester.

The basic brewing process was straightforward. A kiln (**5**) was used to dry and lightly roast the green malt (germinated grain, mainly oats and barley), which was crushed and mixed with water to form the mash. The mash was boiled in large copper basins (**6**), then poured into cooling vats (**7**) before being casked, having yeast added and allowed to ferment (**8**). During the excavation, kilns (**5**), numerous hearths (**6**) and a stone platform (**7**) were uncovered. There was also evidence that pigs were being reared in the plots (**9**), and it is documented that the waste from brewing was often used as pig feed.

Although brewing in this plot ceased by the 15th century, the buildings on Highcross Street remained occupied. Evidence for the foods consumed in the buildings was recovered from numerous rubbish pits and privies. Animal bones show us the various types of meat and fish that were eaten. These included beef, lamb, pork and goose, and to a lesser extent venison, rabbit and duck, whilst fish varied from eel and trout to herring, cod, halibut and even a ray or small shark. Fruit and vegetables were readily available, as the surviving plant seeds show. These included figs, grapes, blackberries, plums and apples, peas, beans and leeks. The main staples of the medieval diet though were cereals such as wheat, rye and barley, which would have been used to make bread and to thicken soups and stews.

Left: Looking across the back yards of houses fronting onto the east side of Highcross Street as they may have been in the 14th century. Excavations show that one property was a brewery producing ale.

Above: These jugs – which came in a huge range of shapes, sizes and decoration – started appearing in Leicester from the 13th century and would have been used to serve ale and wine in homes and inns across the town. They were made at potteries in Leicestershire, Warwickshire, Nottingham and Buckinghamshire and represent the high point of medieval pottery production, in terms of technical expertise and artistry.

The Free Grammar School

The Free Grammar School (**2**) on Highcross Street (**1**) is one of Leicester's most important historic buildings, with a history closely linked to the church of St Peter (**3**). A school providing free education for boys in Leicester was founded in the mid 16th century with a bequest from the estate of William Wygston. Wygston was a prosperous wool merchant who had twice been Mayor of Leicester. The school was initially housed in the south aisle of the church, which by that time was otherwise disused and in a poor state of repair (**4**). One of the church bells was sold to pay for repairs to the church and fitting out one of the aisles as a school room.

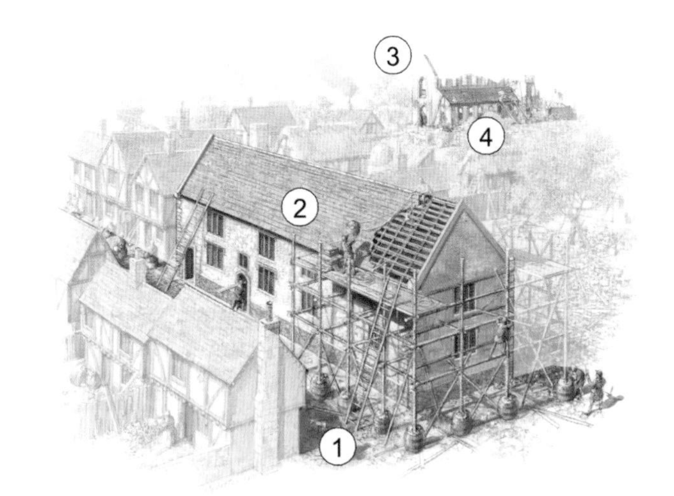

The school was re-founded in 1564 when Queen Elizabeth I made an annual grant of £10 towards the upkeep of the master. As a result the school is often now referred to as Queen Elizabeth's Grammar School. The ageing fabric of St Peter's Church was in a poor state and further repairs were carried out in 1568–9. However, its condition continued to deteriorate and a survey in 1572 noted that the lead had been stripped from the roof and the timbers had been removed from all of the church except the south aisle where the school was housed. In the following year it was decided to dismantle what remained of the church and to use the stone and timber to build a new school. This was to include a classroom for younger boys on the ground floor and another for older boys on the first floor as well as a schoolmaster's house. Construction was completed in 1574.

The town council was responsible for maintaining the school and there are surviving records of expenditure on repairs and alterations up until it closed in 1841. In 1576 the council paid for new desks and seats and for a wooden plaque bearing the Royal arms, whilst in 1775 it paid for new fireplaces at a cost of £10.

During its recent renovation, the Free Grammar School was subject to a detailed survey during which a number of important discoveries were made, including graffiti commemorating its construction and the original stone window surrounds which were still in place hidden beneath modern concrete render. Carved roof timbers were also revealed when the modern ceiling was removed (**right**). These had been reused from the church of St Peter and have been tree-ring dated to the middle of the 15th century.

Fittingly, whilst the school was being restored, St Peter's Church was also being excavated. Stone recovered from the site proved to be ideal for repairs and, more than 430 years after it had been demolished, the church once again provided building materials for the Free Grammar School.

Left: Looking north across Highcross Street, as it may have been in 1574, during the building of the Free Grammar School.

Above: The mid 15th century timber-beam roof inside the Free Grammar School. The timbers came from St Peter's Church.

Acknowledgements

A project on the scale of the Highcross Leicester excavations could not have succeeded without the contribution of many individuals and organisations. University of Leicester Archaeological Services (ULAS) would like to take this opportunity to thank all those involved, especially Hammerson Plc who funded the project, and the many archaeologists and volunteers who contributed to the excavations and the post-excavation analysis. Our thanks also go to Leicester City Council Planning Policy and Design, Leicester Arts and Museums Service and MLA Renaissance for providing grants towards the cost of this publication.

Finally, we would like to extend a special thank you to our artist, Mike Codd, whose beautiful artwork so vividly encapsulates the results of the excavations and brings Leicester's ancient past back to life.

The book was designed and written by Mathew Morris and Richard Buckley with contributions from Jennifer Browning, Hilary Cool, Nick Cooper, Jon Coward, Neil Finn, Tony Gnanaratnam, Harriet Jacklin, Elizabeth Johnson, Tim Higgins, Wayne Jarvis, Angela Monckton, Anita Radini, Deborah Sawday, Gavin Speed, John Tate and Roger Tomlin. We are grateful to Deirdre O'Sullivan, Pam Lowther and Professor Colin Haselgrove of the School of Archaeology and Ancient History, University of Leicester and Chris Wardle of Leicester City Council for their comments on the text, but the authors take full responsibility for any errors or omissions. The site photographs were by ULAS staff, aerials by Webb Aviation and finds photography by Colin Brooks. The reconstruction of Iron Age Leicester on page 15 was by Sarah Geeves, the photograph of the 1930s excavation of Jewry Wall on page 21 was supplied by Leicester Arts and Museums Service and the painting of the interior of the Great Hall of the castle on page 45 is reproduced by kind permission of Joe Goddard.